teacher's friend publications

JUNE

a creative idea book
for the
elementary teacher

written and illustrated
by
Karen Sevaly

edited by
Shelley Price

Copyright © Teacher's Friend,
a Scholastic Company.
www.teachersfriend.com
All rights reserved.
Printed in China.

ISBN 0-439-50375-2

This book is dedicated to teachers and children everywhere.

Table of Contents

Making the most of it!

TF0600 June Idea Book

WHAT IS IN THIS BOOK:

You will find the following in each monthly idea book from Teacher's Friend Publications:

1. A calendar listing every day of the month with a classroom idea and mention of special holidays and events.

2. At least four student awards to be sent home to parents.

3. Three or more bookmarks that can be used in your school library or given to students by you as "Super Student Awards."

4. Numerous bulletin board ideas and patterns pertaining to the particular month and seasonal activity.

5. Easy-to-make craft ideas related to the monthly holidays and special days.

6. Dozens of activities emphasizing not only the obvious holidays, but also the often forgotten celebrations such as Flag Day and International Picnic Day.

7. Creative writing pages, crossword puzzles, word finds, booklet covers, games, paper bag puppets, literature lists and much more!

8. Scores of classroom management techniques and methods proven to motivate your students to improve behavior and classroom work.

HOW TO USE THIS BOOK:

Every page of this book may be duplicated for individual classroom use.

Some pages are meant to be copied or used as duplicating masters. Other pages may be transferred onto construction paper or used as they are.

If you have access to a print shop, you will find that many pages work well when printed on index paper. This type of paper takes crayons and felt markers well and is sturdy enough to last. (Bookmarks work particularly well on index paper.)

Lastly, some pages are meant to be enlarged with an overhead or opaque projector. When we say enlarge, we mean it! Think BIG! Three, four or even five feet is great! Try using colored butcher paper or poster board so you don't spend all your time coloring.

MONTHLY ORGANIZERS:

BULLETIN BOARD IDEAS:

Staying organized month after month, year after year can be a real challenge. Try this simple idea:

After using the loose pages from this book, file them in their own file folder labeled with the month's name. This will also provide a place to save pages from other reproducible books along with craft ideas, recipes and articles you find in magazines and periodicals. (*Essential Pocket Folders* by Teacher's Friend provide a perfect way to store your monthly ideas and reproducibles. Each *Monthly Essential Pocket Folder* comes with a sixteen-page booklet of essential patterns and organizational ideas. There are even special folders for *Back to School*, *The Substitute Teacher* and *Parent-Teacher Conferences*.)

You might also like to dedicate a file box for every month of the school year. A covered box will provide room to store large patterns, sample art projects, certificates and awards, monthly stickers, monthly idea books and much more.

Creating clever bulletin boards for your classroom need not take fantastic amounts of time and money. With a little preparation and know-how, you can have different boards each month with very little effort. Try some of these ideas:

1. Background paper should be put up only once a year. Choose colors that can go with many themes and holidays. The black butcher paper background you used as a spooky display in October will have a special dramatic effect in April with student-made, paper-cut butterflies.

2. Butcher paper is not the only thing that can be used to cover the back of your board. You might also try fabric from a colorful bed sheet or gingham material. Just fold it up at the end of the year to reuse again. Wallpaper is another great background cover. Discontinued rolls can be purchased for a small amount at discount hardware stores. Most can be wiped clean and will not fade like construction paper. (Do not glue wallpaper directly to the board; just staple or pin in place.)

3. Store your bulletin board pieces in large, flat envelopes made from two large sheets of tagboard or cardboard. Simply staple three sides together and slip the pieces inside. (Small pieces can be stored in zip-lock, plastic bags.) Label your large envelopes with the name of the bulletin board and the month and year you displayed it. Take a picture of each bulletin board display. Staple the picture to your storage envelope. Next year when you want to create the same display, you will know right where everything goes. Kids can even follow your directions when you give them a picture to look at.

ADDING THE COLOR:

Putting the color to finished items can be a real bother to teachers in a rush. Try these ideas:

1. On small areas, watercolor markers work great. If your area is rather large, switch to crayons or even colored chalk or pastels.

   (Don't worry, lamination or a spray fixative will keep color on the work and off of you. No laminator or fixative? That's okay, a little hair spray will do the trick.)

2. The quickest method of coloring large items is to start with colored paper. (Poster board, butcher paper or large construction paper work well.) Add a few dashes of a contrasting colored marker or crayon and you will have it made.

3. Try cutting character eyes, teeth, etc. from white typing paper and gluing them in place. These features will really stand out and make your bulletin boards come alive.

   For special effects, add real buttons or lace. Metallic paper looks great on stars and belt buckles, too.

LAMINATION:

If you have access to a roll laminator, then you already know how fortunate you are. They are priceless when it comes to saving time and money. Try these ideas:

1. You can laminate more than just classroom posters and construction paper. Try various kinds of fabric, wallpaper and gift wrapping. You'll be surprised at the great combinations you come up with.

   Laminated classified ads can be used to cut headings for current events bulletin boards. Colorful gingham fabric makes terrific cut letters or bulletin board trim. You might even try burlap! Bright foil gift wrapping paper will add a festive feeling to any bulletin board.

   (You can even make professional looking bookmarks with laminated fabric or burlap. They are great holiday gift ideas for Mom or Dad!)

2. Felt markers and laminated paper or fabric can work as a team. Just make sure the markers you use are permanent and not water-based. Oops, make a mistake! That's okay. Put a little ditto fluid on a tissue, rub across the mark and presto, it's gone! Also, dry transfer markers work great on lamination and can easily be wiped off.

LAMINATION:
(continued)

3. Laminating cut-out characters can be tricky. If you have enlarged an illustration onto poster board, simply laminate first and then cut it out with scissors or an art knife. (Just make sure the laminator is hot enough to create a good seal.)

One problem may arise when you paste an illustration onto poster board and laminate the finished product. If your paste-up is not 100% complete, your illustration and posterboard may separate after laminating. To avoid this problem, paste your illustration onto poster board that measures slightly larger than the illustration. This way, the lamination will help hold down your paste-up.

4. When pasting up your illustration, always try to use either rubber cement, artist's spray adhesive or a glue stick. White glue, tape or paste does not laminate well because it can often be seen under your artwork.

5. Have you ever laminated student-made place mats, crayon shavings, tissue paper collages, or dried flowers? You'll be amazed at the variety of creative things that can be laminated and used in the classroom or as take-home gifts.

PHOTOCOPIES AND
DITTO MASTERS:

Many of the pages in this book can be copied for use in the classroom. Try some of these ideas for best results:

1. If the print from the back side of your original comes through the front when making a photocopy or ditto master, slip a sheet of black construction paper behind the sheet. This will mask the unwanted shadows and create a much better copy.

2. Several potential masters in this book contain instructions for the teacher. Simply cover the type with correction fluid or a small slip of paper before duplicating.

3. When using a new ditto master, turn down the pressure on the duplicating machine. As the copies become light, increase the pressure. This will get longer wear out of both the master and the machine.

4. Trying to squeeze one more run out of that worn ditto master can be frustrating. Try lightly spraying the inked side of the master with hair spray. For some reason, this helps the master put out those few extra copies.

LETTERING AND HEADINGS:

Not every school has a letter machine that produces perfect 4" letters. The rest of us will just have to use the old stencil-and-scissor method. But wait, there is an easier way!

1. Don't cut individual letters as they are difficult to pin up straight, anyway. Instead, hand print bulletin board titles and headings onto strips of colored paper. When it is time for the board to come down, simply roll it up to use again next year. If you buy your own pre-cut lettering, save yourself some time and hassle by pasting the desired statements onto long strips of colored paper. Laminate if possible. These can be rolled up and stored the same way!

Use your imagination! Try cloud shapes and cartoon bubbles. They will all look great.

2. Hand lettering is not that difficult, even if your printing is not up to penmanship standards. Print block letters with a felt marker. Draw big dots at the end of each letter. This will hide any mistakes and add a charming touch to the overall effect.

If you are still afraid to freehand it, try this nifty idea: Cut a strip of poster board about 28" X 6". Down the center of the strip, cut a window with an art knife measuring 20" X 2". There you have it: a perfect stencil for any lettering job. All you need to do is write capital letters with a felt marker within the window slot. Don't worry about uniformity. Just fill up the entire window height with your letters. Move your poster-board strip along as you go. The letters will always remain straight and even because the poster board window is straight.

3. If you must cut individual letters, use construction paper squares measuring 4 1/2" X 6". (Laminate first if you can.) Cut the capital letters as shown. No need to measure; irregular letters will look creative and not messy.

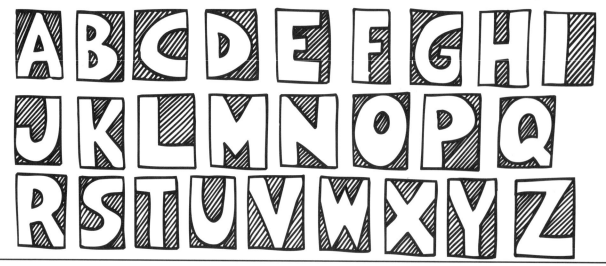

                           TF0600 June Idea Book

Calendar

June

JUNE

1ST American aviator AMELIA EARHART started her last solo flight on this date in 1937. (Ask students to find out more about this courageous woman.)

2ND JOHHNY WEISSMULLER, U.S. swimmer and winner of three Olympic gold medals, was born on this day in 1904. (Mr. Weissmuller also played a famous character in the movies. Ask your students to find out who he portrayed.)

3RD The NEW YORK KNICKERBOCKERS were the first baseball team to appear in uniforms on this day in 1851. They consisted of straw hats, blue pants and white shirts. (Ask your students to design a baseball uniform for their favorite team.)

4TH HENRY FORD test drove the first Ford car on this day in 1896. (Ask your students to find out the name of the car.)

5TH Today is WORLD ENVIRONMENT DAY! (Celebrate this day by talking about ways we can all clean up our environment. Organize a litter clean-up brigade.)

6TH Today is DOUGHNUT DAY! This special day was declared in 1937 by the Salvation Army to raise money during the Great Depression. (Bring in doughnuts for the class and have students write colorful paragraphs describing their favorite doughnut.)

7TH French artist PAUL GAUGUIN was born on this day in 1848. He was famous for his colorful paintings of the island of Tahiti and its people. (Find a print of one of his paintings and display it in the classroom.)

8TH FRANK LLOYD WRIGHT, American architect, was born on this day in 1867. (Ask your students to design a building that they think might best suit the generations of the future.)

9TH American composer and lyricist COLE PORTER was born on this day in 1892. (Play one of his famous pieces during silent reading.)

10TH MAURICE SENDAK, children's author and illustrator, was born on this day in 1928. (Read his book, *Where the Wild Things Are*, to your students in celebration.)

11TH Famous oceanographer and author JACQUES COUSTEAU was born on this day in 1910. (Have your students write an imaginative story about the adventures of his ship, the "Calypso.")

12TH ANNE FRANK, the author of "Diary of a Young Girl," was born on this day in 1929. (Older children may find her story very interesting.)

13TH THURGOOD MARSHALL, the first black Supreme Court Justice, was appointed to the bench on this day in 1967 by President Johnson. (Ask your students to find out the procedures for appointing a Supreme Court Justice.)

14TH Today is FLAG DAY in the United states! (Ask students to list ways we can all show our respect for the American flag.)

15TH Today is SMILE POWER DAY! (Celebrate the day by asking students to tell their favorite joke or write a comical poem or story.)

16TH Soviet cosmonaut VALENTINA TERESHKOVA became the first woman to travel into space in 1963. (Ask students to find out the name of the first U.S. woman astronaut.)

17TH The first REPUBLICAN NATIONAL CONVENTION was held on this day in 1856 in Philadelphia, Pennsylvania. (Ask students to find out the purpose of political conventions, or design a campaign button.)

18TH Today is INTERNATIONAL PICNIC DAY! (Ask each child to bring a sack lunch and visit a local park during the school lunch break.)

19TH The comic strip "Garfield," appeared for the first time on this date in 1978. (Ask your students to create their own comic strip character.)

20TH SAMUEL MORSE was granted a patent for the telegraph on this day in 1840. (Display the Morse Code on the class chalkboard and have students learn to tap out their own names.)

21ST Today marks the first day of SUMMER! It is also the longest day of the year. (Ask older students to find out why this is true.)

22ND On this day in 1970, the VOTING AGE in the United States was changed from 21 years of age to 18. (Have your students' discuss their views on the legal ages for driving, drinking and voting.)

23RD WILMA RUDOLPH, who captured three Olympic gold medals at the 1960 Olympic Games, was born on this day in 1940. (Ask your students to find out more about this talented athlete.)

24TH RADAR was first used on this date in 1930 to detect airplanes. (Ask your students to find what the acronym R-A-D-A-R signifies.)

25TH GEORGE CUSTER and his troops were defeated at the BATTLE OF LITTLE BIGHORN on this day in 1876. (Ask your students to find out what state is the home of this famous battle site.)

26TH On this day in 1870, the world's first BOARDWALK in Atlantic City, New Jersey, opened. (Ask your students to locate Atlantic City on the classroom map.)

27TH HELEN KELLER, American author and lecturer, was born on this date in 1880. (Tell your students about this remarkable woman or read to them from the book *The Miracle Worker.*

28TH The TREATY OF VERSAILLES, which ended World War I, was signed on this day in 1919. (Older children may like to locate Versailles on a European map.)

29TH France annexed the island of TAHITI on this day in 1880. (Ask your students to find Tahiti on the classroom map.)

30TH The FISH AND WILDLIFE SERVICE was established on this day in 1940. (Have your students investigate career opportunities related to this service.)

DON'T FORGET ABOUT THESE OTHER IMPORTANT DAYS!

FATHER'S DAY - The third Sunday in June.

NATIONAL FAMILY DAY - The first Saturday in June.

June

Sunday	Monday	Tuesday	Wednesday	Thursday	Friday	Saturday

TF0600 June Idea Book

June
Activities!

Pencil Toppers

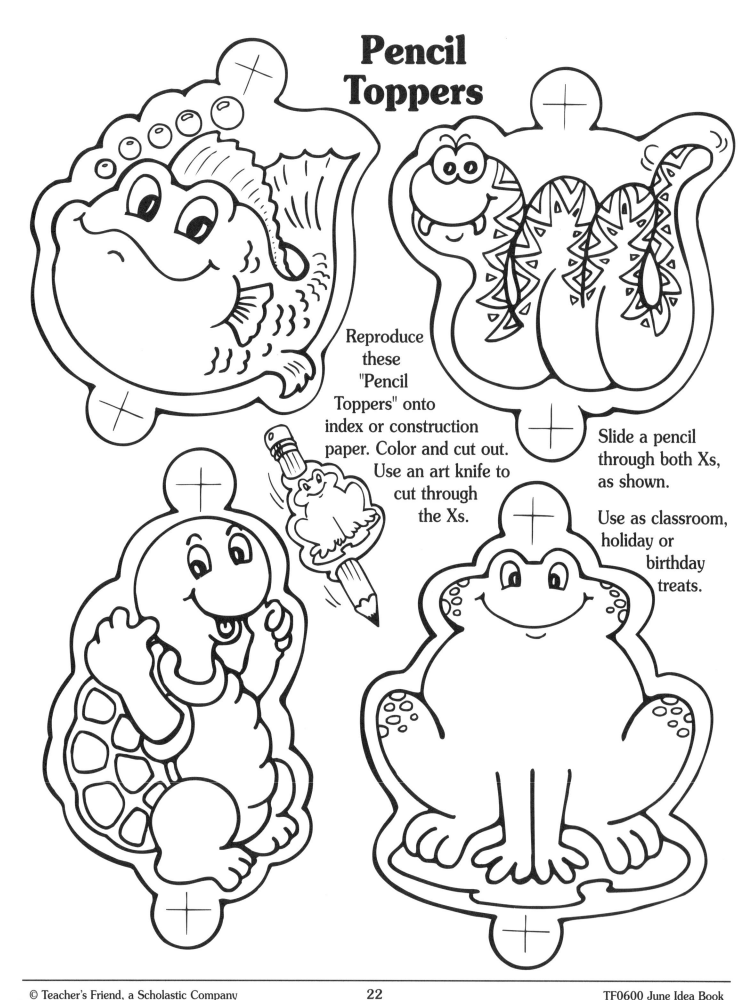

Reproduce these "Pencil Toppers" onto index or construction paper. Color and cut out. Use an art knife to cut through the Xs.

Slide a pencil through both Xs, as shown.

Use as classroom, holiday or birthday treats.

FOR A "WHALE" OF A GOOD TIME... READ A BOOK!

Take a Dive into Reading!

Leap Ahead! ...Read!

Summer Fun!

SUMMER CROSSWORD

COMPLETE THIS SUMMER CROSSWORD PUZZLE.

DOWN

1. A water sport

2. You should always look before you _ _ _ _ into the water.

3. To keep your head above water and remain very still

ACROSS

4. Something wet

5. All swimmers must have strong _ _ _ _.

6. Swimmers kick with their _ _ _ _ _.

7. Someone who watches and saves swimmers

ACTIVITY 1

SUMMER WORD FIND

ACTIVITY 2

FIND THESE SUMMER ACTIVITIES IN THE PUZZLE BELOW:

COOK, BIKE, SLEEP, PICNIC, FISH, CAMP, HIKE, SEW, SKATE, GARDEN, EXPLORE, BOAT, SWIM, PLAY, SPORTS

```
S C V G F S W I M K L O P L K J H F T Y
L A W E D F R S D R F T L D E R F G H Y
E S C O O K S D F G T Y A D S P O R T S
E S W E R A E S W D F R Y W S T Y U I O
P A E D R F W E X P L O R E D T Y U K M
I S W G A R D E N D G T Y H B O A T E R
C W Q E R T Y U A W E R T Y H G F D S T
N F R T Y U H J H D F T Y G H U I J K L
I D R F G T I F F I S H F T Y U I O P V
C B I K E D K V G T Y H N M K I O L R E
A X C G T Y E C A M P D V G T Y H N M J
A W E D S C F R T G B H Y U J M N K I O
A S D F G Y Y H J K I O S K A T E D R T
X C Z V B G F D S A Z X B N M J K H F D
```

TF0600 June Idea Book

Sailboat Pattern

Have students cut the sailboat pattern from colorful paper. Display the boats on the class board. Sails can be cut from white, lined paper in the shape of a triangle and pinned to the sailboats.

Award students with stars or stickers and place them on the boat sails.

Paper nautical flags can be added to the sailboats.

Randy

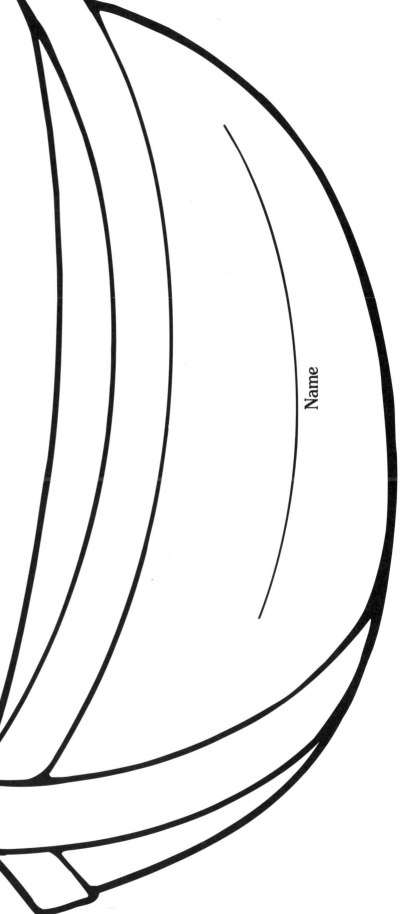

Name

Summer Kids

26

Summer Kids

Water Safety!

It's important to follow safety rules whenever we are around water. It could be a matter of life or death!

- Never swim in areas that are not supervised by an adult or lifeguard.

- Always check to see how deep the water is before going in.

- Always walk, never run, around a pool.

- Never swim during a storm.

- Never swim alone.

- Always wear a flotation device if you are a poor swimmer.

- Do not play rough in the water. Never dunk another person under water.

- Never play in water run-off areas, even if it's sunny outside.

- If you see someone that needs help in the water, yell for help and throw a flotation device to him or her. Do not try to save them yourself unless you have been properly trained.

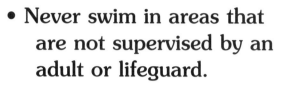

I promise to follow all water safety rules!

_____
Signature

_____
Date

_____
Student's Name

took a "bite" out of learning today!

_____

_____

_____
Date

_____
Teacher

_____
Student's Name

flew high today!

_____   _____
Teacher   Date

_____
Student's Name

caught a lot of praise today!

_____   _____
Teacher   Date

_____
Student's Name

was a "star" student today!

_____
Date

_____
Teacher

Summer Visor

Copy this visor onto sturdy index or construction paper. Children can do the coloring.

Punch holes at both ends and attach string elastic. (With elastic, the students can easily remove the visor without retying.)

If you wish to spare the cost of elastic, simply use mailing string. Either way, the kids will love them and so will you!

I'm Having a Great SUMMER!

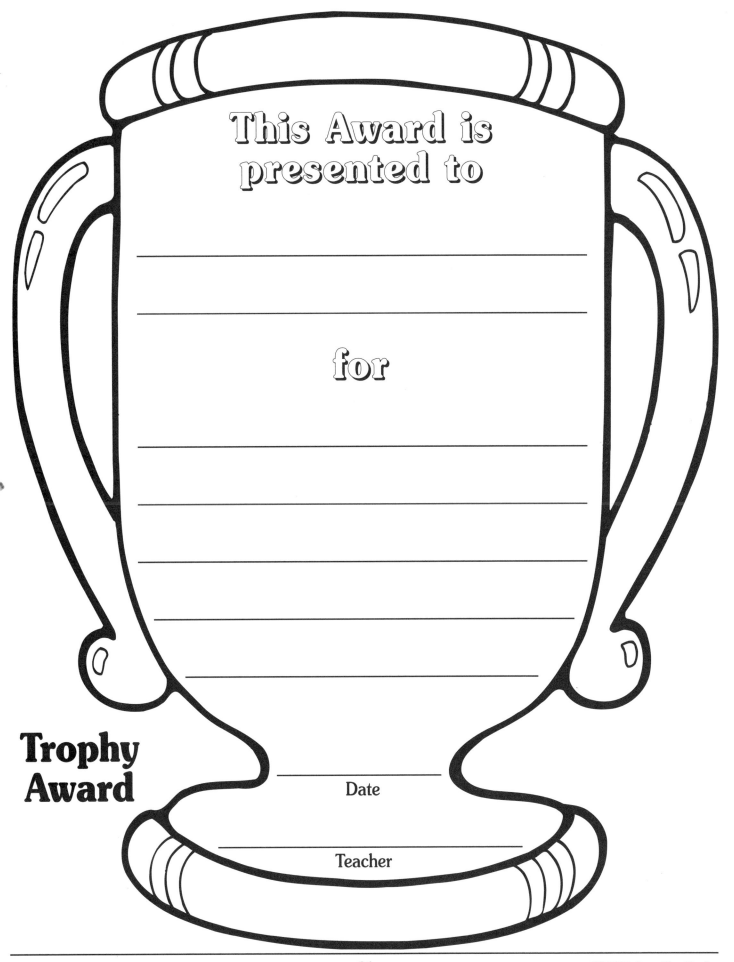

This Award is presented to

_____

_____

for

_____

_____

_____

_____

Trophy Award

_____
Date

_____
Teacher

Star Award

This Award is presented to

_____

for _____

_____

_____

_____

Teacher _____   Date _____

TF0600 June Idea Book

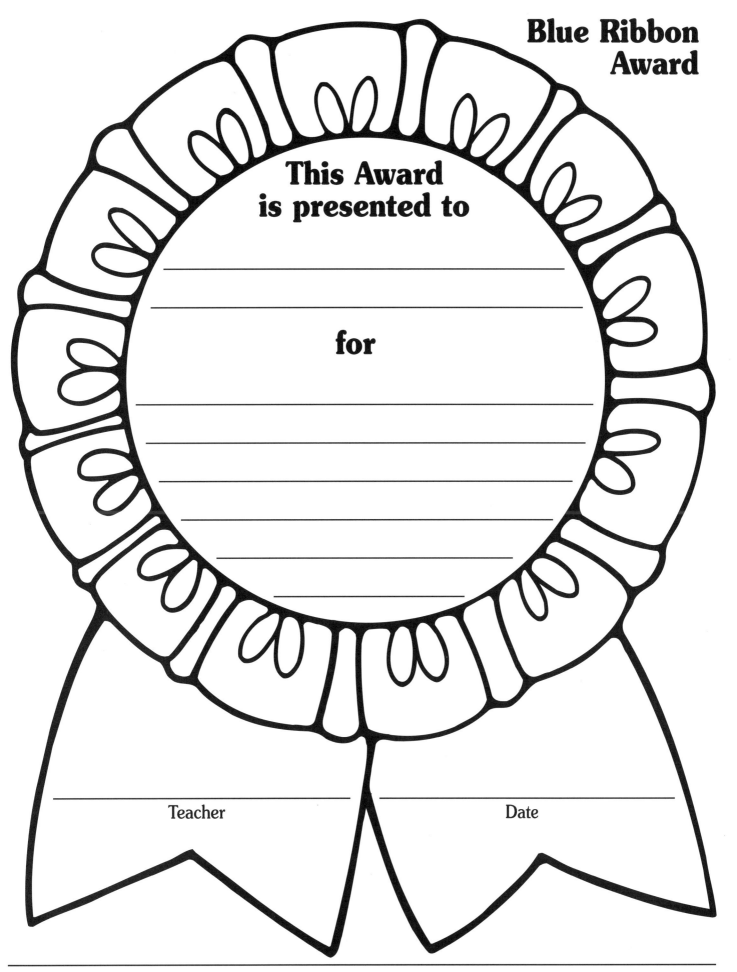

Blue Ribbon
Award

**This Award
is presented to**

for

_____ Teacher   _____ Date

STUDENT
OF THE
MONTH

NAME

SCHOOL

TEACHER

DATE

End of the Year!

Year-End Activities!

The end of the school year often seems to arrive sooner than expected. Try some of these ideas and activities to make those last few days both memorable and productive.

BROWN BAG IT!

During the last few days of school, give each student a large, brown paper grocery bag. Ask each student to decorate his or her bag using crayons, markers, pictures from magazines, etc. Students might like to use the bags to collect fellow students' autographs and phone numbers. On the last day of school, have students use the bag to hold personal items, school work and year-end materials to take home for the summer.

PICK-A-CHORE

Prior to the last day of school, write specific chores that students can do on strips of paper. Students can draw one of the strips and do the specified chore. These could be such tasks as: "Take down the bulletin board display and store it in the box provided," "Erase all of the chalkboards," or "Return all library books to the library." Your classroom will be clean and organized before you know it!

SUMMER POSTCARDS

Students will love creating the postcards you send! Cut cardstock paper into 4" x 6" squares and give one to each student. Instruct them to illustrate the cards using crayons or markers. You may want to suggest a drawing of the school or a mountain or beach scene. When complete, ask students to write their names and complete addresses on individual mailing labels. After the close of school, write a brief note to the students on the backs of the postcards, attach the labels and mail them to your students!

LASTING LETTERS

On the last day before summer break, instruct each student to write a letter to the student that will occupy his or her desk next school year. Encourage them to tell about a variety of classroom events and happenings, including class field trips, a holiday party, the class spelling bee, a favorite story or book, etc. After checking the letters, seal them in envelopes. Before the students arrive on the first day, write the name of each new student on one of the envelopes and place them in the assigned desks. The new kids will be delighted to share with the class the wonderful things they can look forward to from reading the letters.

THANKS FOR THE MEMORIES!

Divide the class into groups of two or three for this positive activity. Assign each group the name of someone at the school that should be recognized by the class. These names can include the school principal, secretary, nurse, cafeteria workers, custodian, playground supervisor and room parents. Instruct each group to design and create a greeting card noting the class's appreciation for their kindness and good work throughout the school year. Students can deliver the cards personally before the end of the day.

TF0600 June Idea Book

Welcome to Grade _____!

You are going to have a great year!

My favorite time in class was

_____

_____

To have a successful year you will need to:

1. _____

_____

2. _____

_____

3. _____

_____

My favorite book to read was _____

_____

The most important rule to follow is _____

_____

My favorite thing to do at recess was _____

_____

Make sure you always _____

_____

Have a great year! I know you will!

_____
Signature

TF0600 June Idea Book

Promotion Certificate!

NAME

has been promoted to

Congratulations!

TEACHER

DATE

TF0600 June Idea Book

Mortarboards

Children will love wearing this simple-to-make mortarboard on the last day of school or during a promotional program.

Cut a long strip of black construction or butcher paper approximately 6" x 22". Wrap the paper around the child's head and staple the ends together to fit.

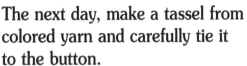

Now, fold the paper in half and cut a "V", as shown, with a pair of scissors. Next, make several cuts along the top edge and fold them outward.

Place a square piece of black posterboard, (about 10" x 10") onto the folded flaps and glue in place. Glue a black button to the center of the mortarboard and let it dry over night.

The next day, make a tassel from colored yarn and carefully tie it to the button.

Promotional Name Tags

Your students will be proud to wear these fun name tags on the last day of school. They are especially meaningful to elementary students who are being promoted to the junior high school.

The students can color them with crayons or markers.

Name

certificate
of
Appreciation

given to

in appreciation for your
valuable contribution of

Our sincere gratitude is extended
to you on this date, _____.

My
_____
Grade
Memory
Book!

Year   School

Teacher

Name

Special People at my School!

School's Name _____

_____

Address _____

_____

Principal _____

Secretary _____

School Nurse _____

Custodian _____

Bus Driver _____

My Teacher _____

Other people who help me at school: _____

_____

_____

_____

_____

_____

My _____ Grade Favorites!

My favorite subject: _____

_____

My favorite book: _____

_____

My favorite lunch: _____

_____

_____

My favorite playground activity: _____

_____

My favorite special event: _____

_____

My best friends: _____

_____

My favorite thing that happened in this grade was: _____

_____

_____

_____

Comments from My Friends!

Signed

Signed

Signed

Signed

Signed

Signed

44

Names, Addresses & Phone Numbers!

Name _____

Address _____

_____

Phone _____

Name _____

Address _____

_____

Phone _____

Name _____

Address _____

_____

Phone _____

Name _____

Address _____

_____

Phone _____

Name _____

Address _____

_____

Phone _____

Name _____

Address _____

_____

Phone _____

Name _____

Address _____

_____

Phone _____

Name _____

Address _____

_____

Phone _____

In _____ Grade,

I was _____ years old!

I was _____ inches tall!

I wore size _____ shoes!

I had freckles ☐ yes ☐ no

I wore glasses ☐ yes ☐ no

I wore braces ☐ yes ☐ no

My favorite thing to wear
to school was:

_____

_____

Comments From
My Teacher:

My School
Picture!

Signed

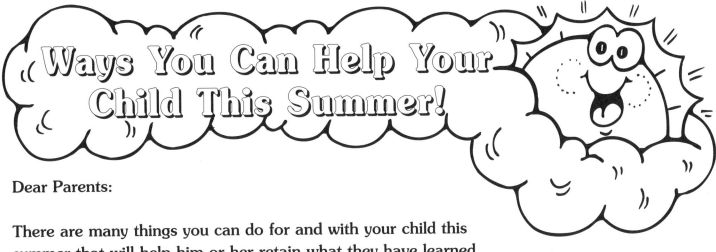

Ways You Can Help Your Child This Summer!

Dear Parents:

There are many things you can do for and with your child this summer that will help him or her retain what they have learned during this school year. Here are a few ideas:

- Make regular visits to the public library and encourage your child to read daily.
- Visit local museums and cultural centers. Encourage an on-going discussion of what was seen and what your child learned from the visit.

- See that your child gets regular physical exercise. Sign them up for swimming lessons, karate lessons, dance lessons or encourage them to join a team sport.

- Limit your child to a minimum amount of television viewing. Always make sure that children only watch programs that are appropriate for their age and maturity level.

- Arrange several opportunities when you can help your child review math facts and spelling words. You might want to purchase or make simple flash cards. If you make the activity fun, it will be an enjoyable time for both you and your child.

- Encourage your child to take up a hobby. You might suggest and provide the materials for an art activity or a cooking project. A child that likes to sing may enjoy joining a junior choir or children's drama group. You might want to encourage your child to start a collection such as rocks, insects, shells, pressed flowers, marbles, etc.

- Provide a new notebook or blank book that your child can use as a daily journal. Suggest a specific time each day in which he or she can write about the day's events or personal feelings. Encourage good penmanship, spelling and punctuation.

- Read to your child every day. Provide a time before bed to read a story together or you may want to read a short, funny story, poem or news article at the dinner table. The *Reader's Digest Magazine* is an excellent source of short, concise and often humorous stories that family members can read to each other.

- Spend some quiet time each day talking to your child about the things that are important to him or her. Make sure that you take time for hugs and kisses and to affirm your child of your love and admiration for their special qualities.

An End of the Year Letter to My Teacher!

Date _____

Dear _____

_____

_____

_____

_____

_____

_____

_____

_____

_____

_____

_____

_____

_____
Signed

Flag Day!

Flag Day!

On Sunday, June 14, 1885, a young schoolmaster named Bernard Cigrand held a birthday party for the 108th birthday of the American flag.

All the people in his hometown of Waubeka, Wisconsin, were invited to the celebration. The school house was decorated with the colors red, white and blue and homemade flags were displayed everywhere. His pupils, dressed in their Sunday best, recited patriotic poems and told stories about the American flag. A poem by Francis Scott Key entitled "The Star-Spangled Banner" was also included. A large cake was served along with refreshing lemonade. At the end of the celebration, everyone joined in a pledge of loyalty to the flag.

After this special day, Cigrand devoted a great deal of his time to reminding people to honor our flag. He wrote letters to statesmen and made numerous speeches. He became known as the "father" of Flag Day.

In 1916, President Woodrow Wilson officially proclaimed June 14th to be observed throughout the United States as "Flag Day." Every year since that time, flags have been flown on all civic buildings and many schools participate in special programs. It's a time to honor our country's symbol and to feel proud to be an American.

THE HISTORY OF THE U.S. FLAG

The original flag of the United States was raised for the first time on June 14, 1777. It consisted of thirteen stripes, representing the original thirteen colonies, and thirteen stars, one for each state in the union.

After the signing of the Declaration of Independence in 1776, the Continental Congress decided that a national flag was needed to symbolize the unity of their new country.

According to legend, a committee led by George Washington requested a woman from Philadelphia named Betsy Ross to design and make the first United States flag. It is believed that it was she who chose the colors red, white and blue. Later these colors became a part of the Great Seal of the United States. It is said that the color red stands for courage and hardiness, white symbolizes purity and innocence and blue represents perseverance and justice.

Respecting the American Flag!

1. The flag should always be treated in a respectful manner.

2. Always stand when the flag is represented in a parade or carried in an honor guard. Hats should also be removed when the flag is presented.

3. The flag should only be flown from sunrise to sunset. It may be flown at night only when it is properly lighted.

4. The flag should be stored and displayed in a way that will keep it clean, dry and free from harm. It should never be displayed in extremely bad weather.

5. The flag must always be kept from touching the floor or the ground.

6. The flag must never be used as a decoration or a costume.

7. Nothing should ever be placed on or above the flag.

8. When the flag is displayed in a window or on a wall, always keep the union of stars to the top and the observer's left. The flag is only flown upside down as a distress signal, a call for help.

9. When the flag becomes worn beyond repair, destroy it in a dignified manner by burning it.

10. When displaying the flag on a flag pole, always raise the flag quickly to the top of the pole and lower it slowly.

11. When a famous person passes away, the flag is often displayed at half-mast. Hoist the flag to the top of the pole and slowly lower it to half-mast. When it is time to take it down, raise the flag again to the the top of the pole and bring it down slowly. It always takes two people to raise or lower the flag correctly.

FOLDING OUR FLAG

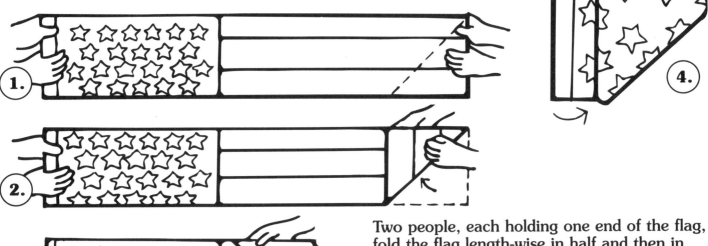

Two people, each holding one end of the flag, fold the flag length-wise in half and then in quarters. The person holding the striped end makes a triangular fold. He or she continues folding the flag in triangles until only the union of the stars is showing.

"Old Glory" - 1777 to Present

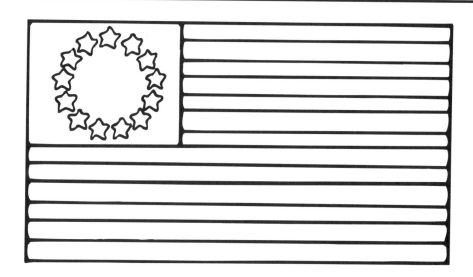

FIRST OFFICIAL FLAG - JUNE 14, 1777

The Continental Congress created a resolution that states: "The flag of the United States shall be 13 stripes, alternating red and white, and the union be 13 stars, white in a blue field, representing the new constellation." This flag is also known as the "Betsy Ross" flag.

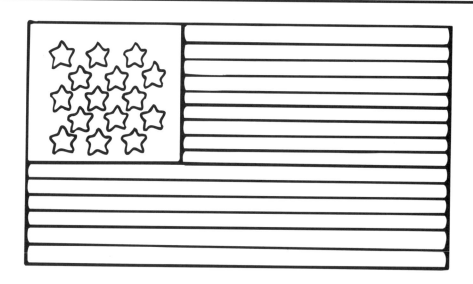

THE FIFTEEN STRIPE FLAG - 1794

On January 13, 1794, the Congress recognized the new states of Vermont and Kentucky and voted to add two stripes and two stars to the flag. This is the flag that inspired Francis Scott Key to write the American National Anthem. This flag remained unchanged until 1818.

"Old Glory" - 1777 to Present

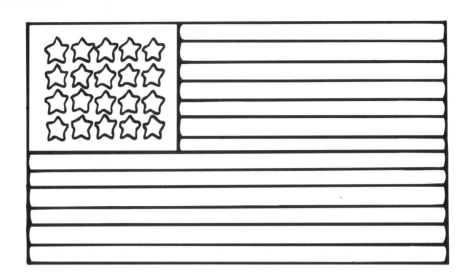

THE NATIONAL FLAG OF 1818

Twenty states had joined the Union by 1818. On April 18th, the Congress voted to have the flag display 13 alternating red and white stripes representing the original 13 states and each new state would be recognized by adding a new star.

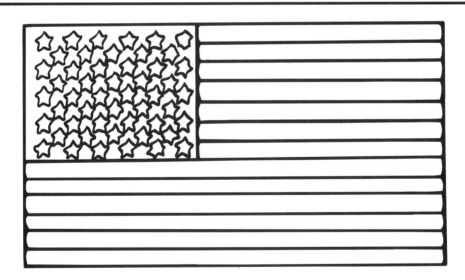

OUR PRESENT NATIONAL FLAG

The flag steadily changed between 1818 and 1912 as more states were added to the Union. From 1912 to 1959, there were 48 stars on the blue field. Alaska became our 49th state in 1959 and then in 1960 Hawaii became our 50th state. With 50 stars and 13 stripes, "Old Glory" as we know it, came into being.

The Flag of the United States of America!

TF0600 June Idea Book

The Meaning of the Pledge of Allegiance!

I PLEDGE	I PROMISE
ALLEGIANCE	TO BE LOYAL (We will respect our flag and be loyal and true to our country.)
TO THE FLAG	TO OUR COUNTRY'S SYMBOL (The flag always reminds us of our country.)
OF THE UNITED STATES OF AMERICA	OF OUR COUNTRY (The United States of America is the name of our country.)
AND TO THE REPUBLIC FOR WHICH IT STANDS	AND TO THE GOVERNMENT OF OUR COUNTRY (A republic is a government in which the people elect their leaders.)
ONE NATION UNDER GOD	OUR ONE COUNTRY WHICH BELIEVES IN GOD (The term "nation" is another word for "country.")
INDIVISIBLE	CANNOT BE DIVIDED (Our country is one which cannot be separated or divided.)
WITH LIBERTY	WITH FREEDOM (In America, we believe that all people should have the same rights. We have many freedoms including freedom of speech, religion and peaceable assembly.)
AND JUSTICE FOR ALL.	AND FAIRNESS TO EVERYONE. (Each person is to follow the laws of our country. If someone breaks the law, they will be given time to show that he or she did no wrong.)

The Flag and the Pledge of Allegiance!

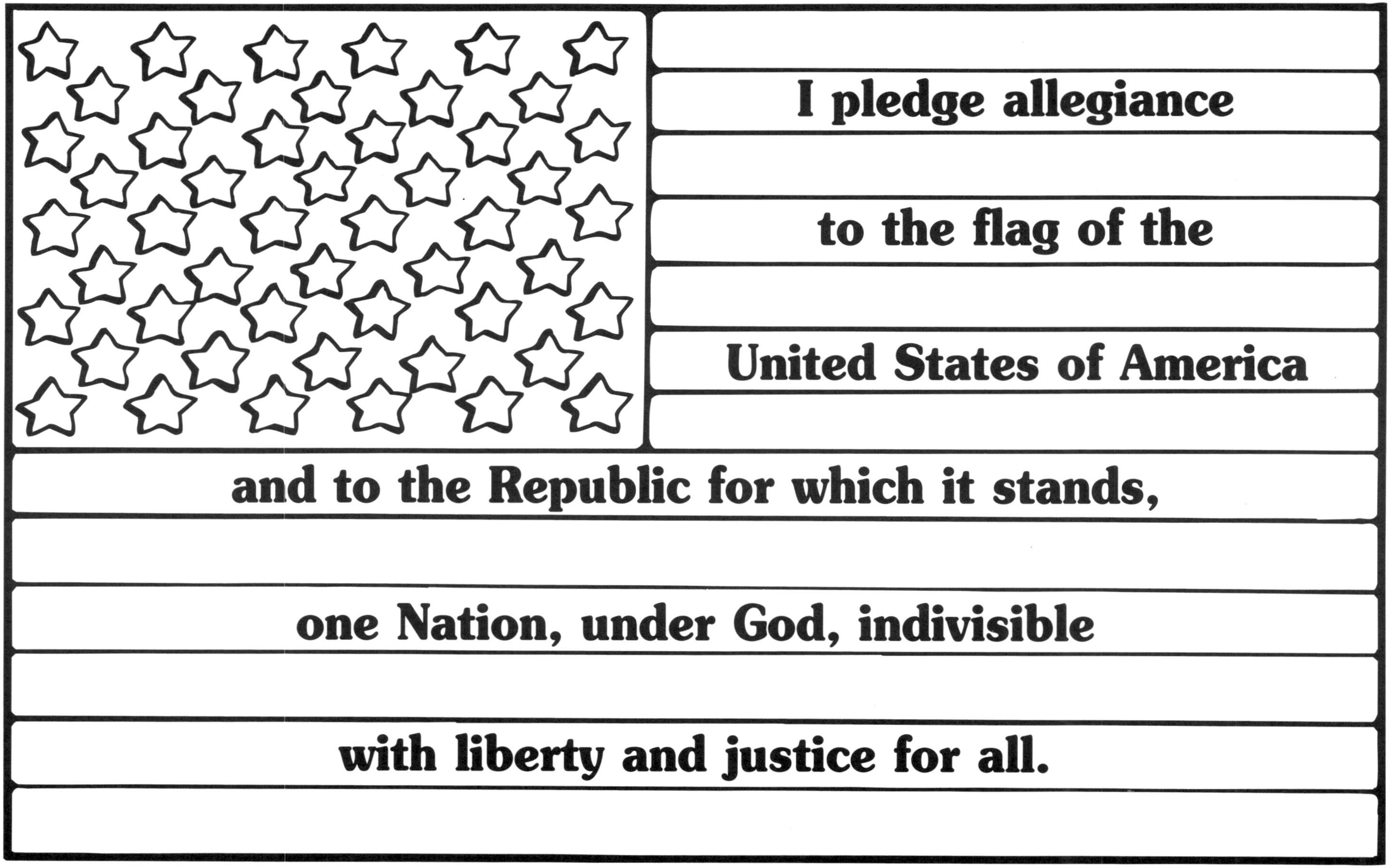

I pledge allegiance

to the flag of the

United States of America

and to the Republic for which it stands,

one Nation, under God, indivisible

with liberty and justice for all.

The Pledge of Allegiance!

I pledge allegiance

to the flag of the

United States of America

Assemble the "Stars and Stripes" to form the United States flag.

Cut the Pledge of Allegiance stripes from white paper and the other seven stripes from red paper. Cut the star field from white paper and color it blue with white stars.

and to the Republic for which it stands,

one Nation, under God, indivisible

with liberty and justice for all.

TF0600 June Idea Book

Why I'm Proud to be an American!

_____

Student's Name

_____

_____

_____

_____

_____

_____

_____

_____

_____

_____

_____

_____

Father's Day!

My Dad's the Greatest!

Father's Day!

In 1909, Louise Smart Dodd of Spokane, Washington, encouraged the congregation of her church to devote a special day to fathers. Louise was very close to her father. Her mother had died when Louise was a small child and her father had lovingly raised her and her five brothers. Louise wanted to honor her father by dedicating a special day to all fathers.

Several years later, President Coolidge recommended that a "Father's Day" be nationally observed. The third Sunday in June was selected for this special day. Today, children in both Canada and the United States honor their fathers with gifts and cards. It is customary to wear a red or white rose in respect for one's father on Father's Day.

#1 Dad Badge!

Give your dad his own special badge to wear on Father's Day!

You might like to pin the badge to the inside of a card you give him on his special day!

#1 DAD!

LOVE,

_____

My Dad is Special!

_____

My Dad is special because...

_____

_____

_____

_____

I like it when my Dad _____

_____

_____

I like to make my Dad smile by _____

_____

_____

My Dad's favorite thing to do is _____

_____

My Dad is smart! He even knows _____

_____

_____

_____

I think my Dad is _____**!**

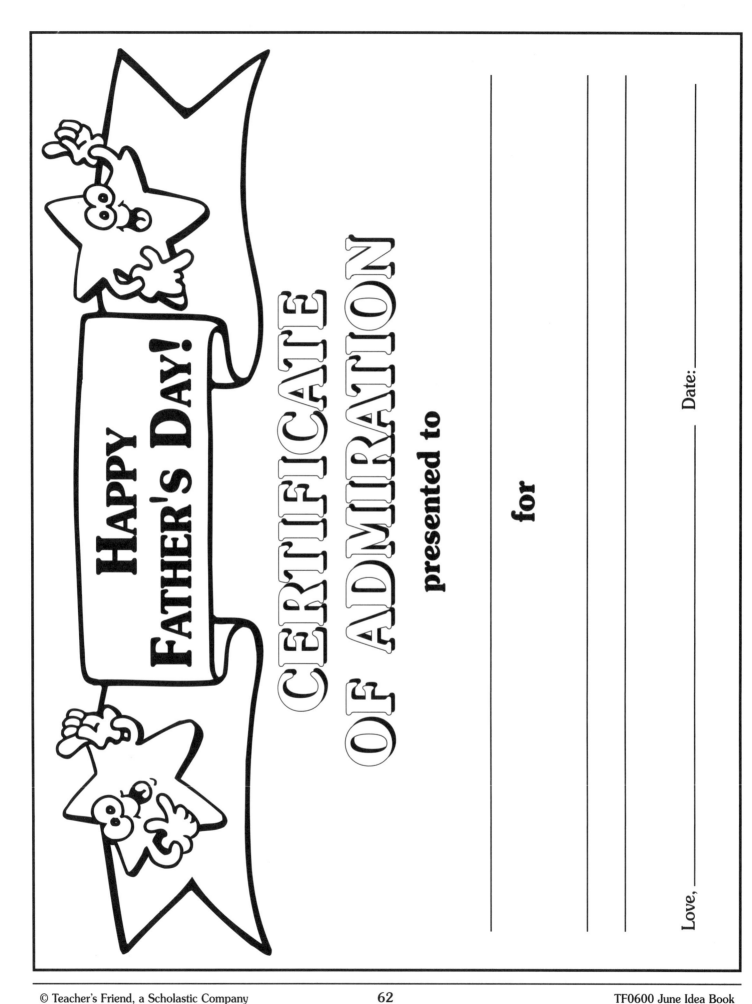

HAPPY FATHER'S DAY!

CERTIFICATE OF ADMIRATION

presented to

for

Date:

Love,

Keys for Dad!

Cut this key pattern from colored paper and encourage students to fill in the information. Some ideas include: "I promise to sweep the garage." "I promise to rake the leaves." "I promise to not hit my sister."

Punch holes in the keys and tie them together with a length of yarn. Students can give the "Key Chains" to their dads on Father's Day!

Happy Father's Day!
"You've got the key to my heart!"

Signed

In celebration of your special day
I promise to:

A Briefcase for Dad!

FOLD

Cut this briefcase pattern from brown paper. Write a message to Dad inside. Fold where indicated, cut out below the handle and insert the latch to make the briefcase close.

FOLD

Cut Out.

Cards for Dad!

Children love giving their fathers and/or grandfathers gifts and cards on Father's Day. Here are a few ideas.

DAD'S TIE!
Give each student a long strip of patterned wallpaper. (You can often find damaged rolls at a reduced price at your neighborhood hardware or paint store.) Have them fan-fold the paper as shown and instruct them to cut a "V" at one end. Trim it with scissors. Father's Day messages to Dad can be written down the tie.

DAD'S PORTRAIT!
Draw a picture of Dad on a folded sheet of construction paper. You might want to draw his portrait on a small paper plate and paste it to the folded paper. Add a bow tie cut from gift wrap paper or wallpaper, yarn for his hair and glue real buttons onto his shirt. Write your own Father's Day greeting inside.

DAD'S IN THE NEWS!
Paste a sheet from the local newspaper to a sheet of construction paper. (If your dad likes sports, use the Sports section. If he enjoys business news, use the Business section.) Use a bold, red marking pen to write the caption, "Dad, You're in the News..." Inside, tell him that you think he's the greatest dad ever and more important than any famous celebrity or world politician!

Father's Day Pocket!

Make a Father's Day gift by cutting a pocket from construction paper. Glue or staple three edges of the pocket together.

Write special notes or list various chores on the pencil, pen and ruler that you would like to do for your dad on this special day. Place these things inside the pocket and give it to him on Father's Day!

FOLD

Happy Father's Day!

LOVE:

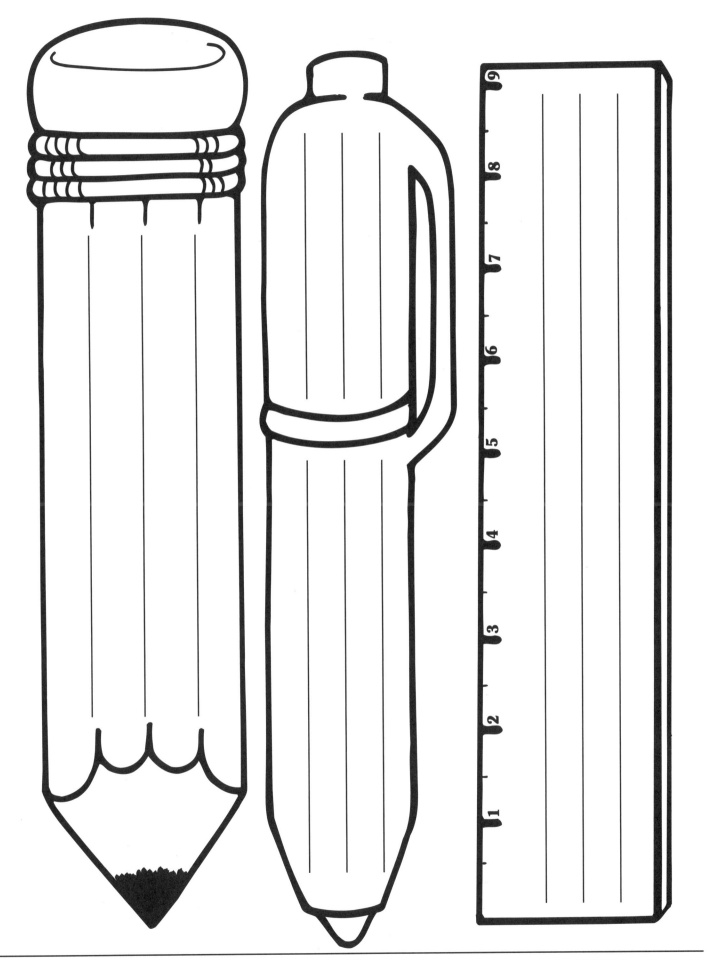

Father's Day Creative Writing

Write a sentence for each letter in the word "Father."

F

A

T

H

E

R

My definition of a great Dad!

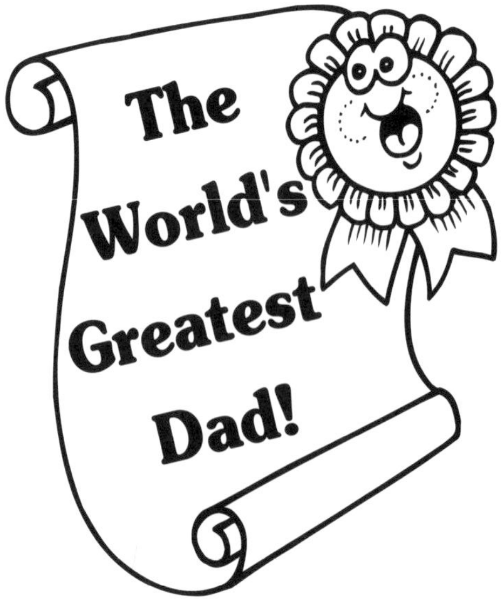

The World's Greatest Dad!

Frogs, Turtles, Snakes & Gators!

Tadpoles to Frogs!

Raising tadpoles (or polywogs) in the classroom is fairly easy, educational and really fun for your students.

During the early part of summer, you can find tadpole eggs at the edges of water ponds. The eggs look like transparent jelly. Yet if you look closely, you'll see tiny tadpoles inside, ready to hatch. Newly hatched tadpoles can be found near water weeds, most often in July or August.

Catch the tadpoles in a large can. Quietly lay the can sideways in the water and the tadpoles should swim in. Make sure you also use a second can to transport green pond scum and some small water plants. It's best if you have the pond nearby so you can replenish the pond water often.

Once home, line the bottom of a large jar, fish bowl or tank with mud or sand. Place water plants in the mud, securing them with stones. Build an island with stones for the developing frogs to climb. Add the pond water, scum and tadpoles.

Every few days, replace the water with new pond water. Tadpoles eat the algae in the water. You can also feed them tiny bits of spinach, hard-boiled egg or soft-bodied insects. (You may use tap water if you let it stand for 48 hours.)

Your tadpole's changes will be dramatic. Here is what to look for:

• When a tadpole first hatches, it breathes with gills. After a few days, its mouth opens and so does a breathing hole at the side of the head.

• Small suckers appear on the underside of the tadpoles. They use them to hold tight to things in the water. After a few days the suckers disappear and the tadpoles begin swimming.

• Notice two small bumps near the tadpole's tail. These will become hind legs.

• Look for two more bumps, one at the breathing hole and the second on the other side of the head. These will become the frog's front legs. Notice that the tadpole is beginning to breathe water in and out of its mouth. Soon it will begin climbing out of the water to use its lungs instead of gills.

• The tail is starting to disappear. During this time the tadpole uses its tail for nutrition and won't need other food for awhile.

When your tadpoles become tiny frogs, return them to the pond. There they will live a much happier life and benefit us by eating pesky insects!

Tadpoles to Frogs!

Your students will love observing the life cycle of the frog in the classroom. Tadpoles can be raised in a glass aquarium. Later, when the frogs have fully developed, you will want to build a vivarium.

Your vivarium can be built with a wooden frame measuring about four feet long, two feet wide and two feet high. The box should be covered with a fine wire screen. Place your vivarium outside in a semi-shaded area. It should contain a good supply of water. (A kitchen dish-pan, filled with pond water, will work fine.) Make sure to include plenty of rocks, small logs, and green plants to provide shelter for the frogs. You might have to collect insects for your frogs to eat.

Frog Activities!

FROGS AND TOADS

Ask your students to find out the difference between a frog and a toad. The clue is to look at the skin.

Frogs have shiny skin. Toads have dull skin. Frogs have smooth skin. Toads have bumps.

The bumps on a toad's skin are actually glands. They protect the toad from predators by emitting a terrible-tasting liquid. Creatures thinking about eating a toad soon have an unpleasant surprise. This gives the old story about the princess that kisses a frog, hoping it will become a handsome prince, a new meaning. She would really have second thoughts if it were a toad!

FROG VOCABULARY

Ask your students to find the meanings of these words and use them in a story about frogs.

amphibians	polliwogs
tadpole	eggs
hatch	bullfrog
croak	lily pad
swamp	pond
insects	gills
tail	jump
leap	frog
jelly	algae

FROG STORY STARTERS

Try some of these story starter ideas with your class:

- Our Town Was Invaded By Frogs!
- The Frog That Grew To Be 500 Pounds!
- I Found a Frog in My Bathtub!
- The Prince that Turned into a Frog!
- The Tadpole That Never Became a Frog!
- Frog Legs for Dinner!
- The Frog That Could Jump a Mile!

Frog Facts!

Frogs and toads may look alike but it's easy to tell them apart. Frogs have smooth, slippery, soft skin. Toads have rough, warty skin.

Frogs and toads are amphibians. This means that they live both on land and in the water.

The mother frog lays her eggs near vegetation in a pond of water.

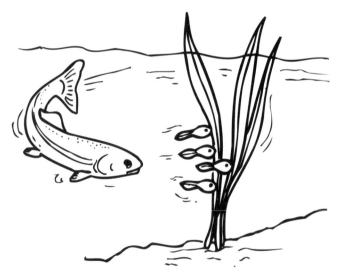

The eggs hatch into tiny tadpoles that breathe with gills and feed on plants in the water.

Frog Facts!

Tadpoles become fast swimmers, using their fish-like tail to propel them through the water.

Soon the tadpoles begin to change. Small back legs are the first to appear. Next, the front legs begin to develop.

As the tadpoles grow, the tails become shorter and shorter. At last the change is complete.

From now on, the new little frog will spend some of its time on land. Now, its main source of food is insects.

TF0600 June Idea Book

Name

FOLD

**Frog
Booklet**

 TF0600 June Idea Book

Frog and Lily Pad

Use these frog and lily pad patterns to create a variety of matching activities.

Name

You might want to place several lily pads across the class bulletin board. Label each one with a task that each student needs to complete. Give all students a paper frog labeled with their names. "Jump" the frogs from pad to pad as the tasks are completed.

TF0600 June Idea Book

Frog "Jumper"!

Spring

Cut Out

Cut Out

Cut Out

Cut Out

Cut Out

Cut Out

Cut Out

Cut Out

Color and cut these two patterns from card stock.

Cut out the circles from the "spring" pattern. Fold like an accordion.

Make a crease down the fold line of the "jumper" pattern. Thread the jumper stem through the holes in the spring. Pull down on the bottom handle of the jumper while holding the lowest notch of the spring. Release the jumper to see the frog jump!

FOLD

Jumper

Frog Puppet

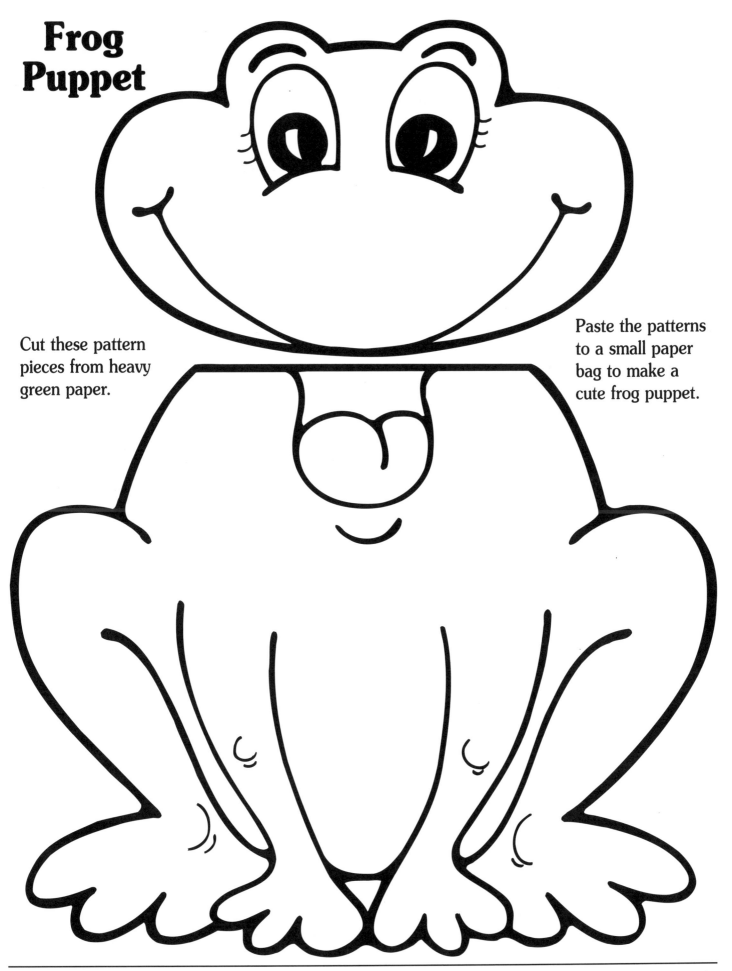

Cut these pattern pieces from heavy green paper.

Paste the patterns to a small paper bag to make a cute frog puppet.

TF0600 June Idea Book

Leaping Gameboard

TEACHERS: Two, three or four children can play this game. Make your own task cards or write math problems, that must be solved, on each space.

Help the frogs get to land!

TF0600 June Idea Book

Reptile or Amphibian?

_____
Student's Name

The name of my animal is:

_____

It is: ☐ a reptile   ☐ an amphibian

It can be found _____

_____

The life cycle of this animal is interesting. Here's how:

_____

_____

This animal feeds on: _____

_____

Some interesting facts about this animal are:

_____

_____

_____

_____

_____

_____

A Drawing of My Animal!

Reptile and Amphibian Fun!

ACTIVITY 3   UNSCRAMBLE THESE REPTILE AND AMPHIBIAN WORDS!

leturt   _ _ _ _ _ _

skena   _ _ _ _ _

grof   _ _ _ _

adot   _ _ _ _

toraglila   _ _ _ _ _ _ _ _ _

zildar   _ _ _ _ _ _

colideroc   _ _ _ _ _ _ _ _ _

trtooise   _ _ _ _ _ _ _ _

ACTIVITY 4   ANSWER THESE QUESTIONS.

1. Frogs start life as __ __ __ __ __ __ __ .

2. Frogs and toads are __ __ __ __ __ __ __ __ __ __ __ .

3. Most water turtles are __ __ __ __ eaters.

4. Land turtles are __ __ __ __ __ eaters.

5. Some tortoises can live to be __ __ __ years old.

6. All turtles lay __ __ __ __ .

7. All reptiles are __ __ __ __ -blooded.

8. Snakes have no __ __ __ __ .

9. Turtles, crocodiles, lizards and snakes are __ __ __ __ __ __ __ __ .

This is what I've learned about reptiles and amphibians:

_____

_____

_____

_____

Turtle Activities!

Turtles and tortoises are fascinating animals. They are some of the oldest on earth. Scientists have found fossils dating as far back as 2,000 years ago. That means that turtles and tortoises survived the extinction of the dinosaurs. Try some of these activities with your students.

REPTILE AWARENESS

Begin your study of turtles by explaining to your students the differences between reptiles and mammals. Continue to explain that there are four major categories of reptiles. Write these across the top of the class board: turtles, snakes, lizards and crocodilians. Ask students to find out unique characteristics of each type of reptile, such as turtles having a shell and laying eggs in the sand or snakes swallowing their food whole.

You may wish to ask a pet store owner or someone that has several reptiles to come to the classroom and share his or her experiences. Children will love seeing and feeling a variety of friendly reptiles.

TORTOISE OR TURTLE

Have your students investigate the differences between a tortoise and a turtle. (All tortoises are turtles but a tortoise lives only on land, usually in dry climates, and turtles live both in the water and on land.)

Students may like to find out the names and habitats of the more common turtles and tortoises and write a report. Here is a list of some turtles to research:

Box Turtle	Painted Turtle
Green Turtle	Leopard Turtle
Snapping Turtle	Soft-Shelled Turtle
Galapagos Turtle	Musk Turtle
Sea Turtle	Desert Turtle
Gopher Turtle	Leatherback Turtle

SELF-PROTECTION

Turtles are the only reptile with a shell. Most turtles can pull their heads, tails and legs into their shells for protection. (Sea turtles cannot withdraw their heads or legs.)

Brainstorm with your students on other ways different animals protect themselves from predators. Ask them to imagine if humans had some of these same abilities. What if we had shells and could pull in our heads, arms and legs? Or, what if we could change colors, matching our surroundings? Students may like to write a creative story about this subject.

TURTLE READING

Give each student a copy of a turtle pattern complete with sectioned shell. On the class board write several subject areas you wish them to read that will broaden their interests in the library, such as biography, sports, legends and folk tales, etc. Color code each of these subjects. As students read a book from a selected area, they color a section of the turtle's shell the appropriate color. Books are read and the activity continues until the turtles all have multi-colored shells.

Turtle Pattern

TF0600 June Idea Book

Turtle Facts!

There are many different kinds of turtles. However, they all have one thing in common: a shell. This is the one thing that makes them unique to other reptiles.

Some turtles live in water and some on land. Land turtles are often called tortoises. They can live to be a hundred years old and can grow to more than one thousand pounds.

Most water turtles are meat eaters. They feed on small fish. The land turtles are vegetarians and eat only plants.

A box turtle can pull his head, legs and tail into his shell, completely protecting himself.

TF0600 June Idea Book

Turtle Facts!

If a box turtle gets turned upside down, it has a very hard time turning itself over again.

All turtles lay their eggs on land. The mother digs a hole in soft dirt or sand. She lays her eggs in the hole and them covers them with dirt.

The mother turtle then leaves her eggs to incubate in the warm sunshine, never to return.

The eggs hatch in about three months. The little turtles have to struggle to break through the tough shells of the eggs.

Turtle Craft

Cut these patterns from heavy paper. Cut two slits along the dotted lines on the turtle's shell.

Slide the body through the shell. To make the turtle's head stick out or go in, simply push or pull the tail.

Write a message on the turtle's body that is only revealed when you pull the tail.

TF0600 June Idea Book

Turtle
Paper Bag
Puppet

Cut these patterns
from colored paper
and paste them to a
small paper bag to
make a cute turtle
puppet.

Snakes!

Unlike other reptiles, snakes have no legs. Instead, they walk with their ribs. A snake has many small bones that connect together to form the backbone. Therefore, they can bend it very easily. By wiggling from side to side, a snake travels with ease.

All reptiles, including snakes, are cold-blooded. This means that their temperature rises and falls with the temperature of the air around them. You can often find snakes sunning themselves on rocks in the springtime. This is their way of raising the temperature of their bodies.

Like all reptiles, snakes shed their skin periodically. How often they shed their skin depends on their age, diet and overall health. Snakes shed their skin in one long piece. They crawl out of their old skin, turning it inside out as they go. Young snakes shed their skin more often than older ones because they are growing.

Most snakes are very helpful to humans because they eat small rodents like rats and mice. They also eat harmful insects. The king snake will even eat other poisonous snakes. Snakes search for their food by feeling for vibrations in the ground. They also smell with their tongues. Snakes have poorly developed sight and hearing.

Most snakes hatch their young from eggs, but a few types bear their young live. The garter snake is one of these. The mother garter snake carries her eggs in her body until they develop into baby snakes. She then delivers them alive.

Fully grown snakes vary from only a few inches long to more than 30 feet. The anaconda is the largest snake known, measuring as long as 38 feet and weighing more than 250 pounds.

Snakes are most commonly found in the warm areas of the world. Where it is cold, snakes must seek protection and hibernate in the winter.

Ask your students to research the following questions:
- Why do snakes stick out their tongues?
- Why do most snakes live underground?
- Why do snakes shed their skin?
- How can snakes swallow something larger than their heads?
- How are snakes useful to humans?
- Name three poisonous snakes.

Happy Snake!

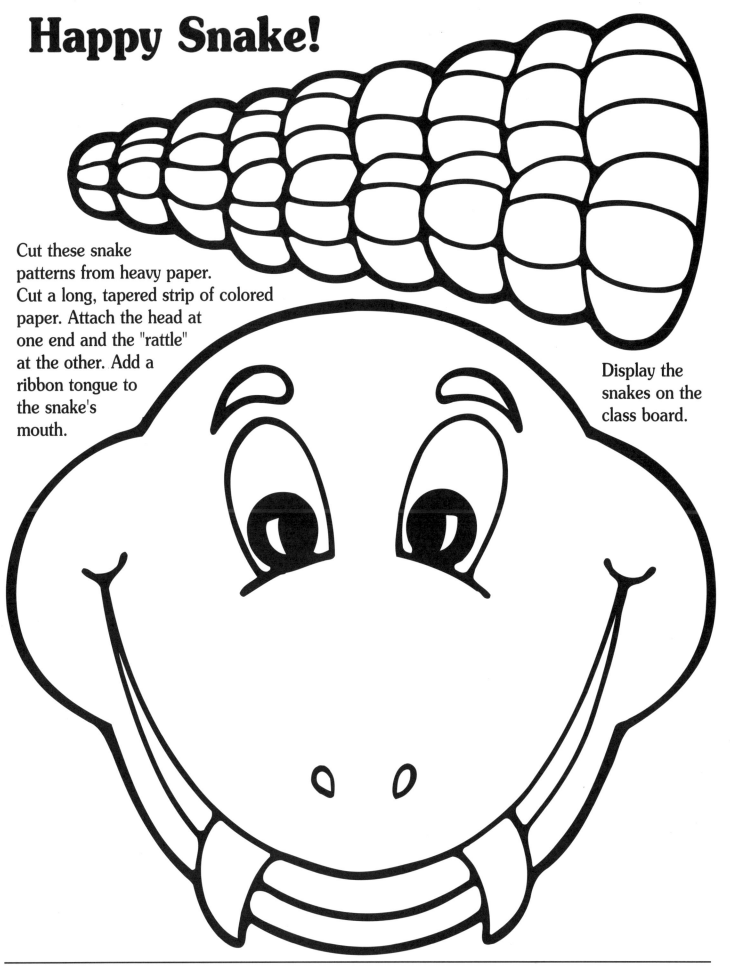

Cut these snake patterns from heavy paper. Cut a long, tapered strip of colored paper. Attach the head at one end and the "rattle" at the other. Add a ribbon tongue to the snake's mouth.

Display the snakes on the class board.

TF0600 June Idea Book

Snake Trail

Teachers: Use this snake as a gameboard with your own task cards or have students color in one section of the snake each time they accomplish a goal.

Standing Alligator

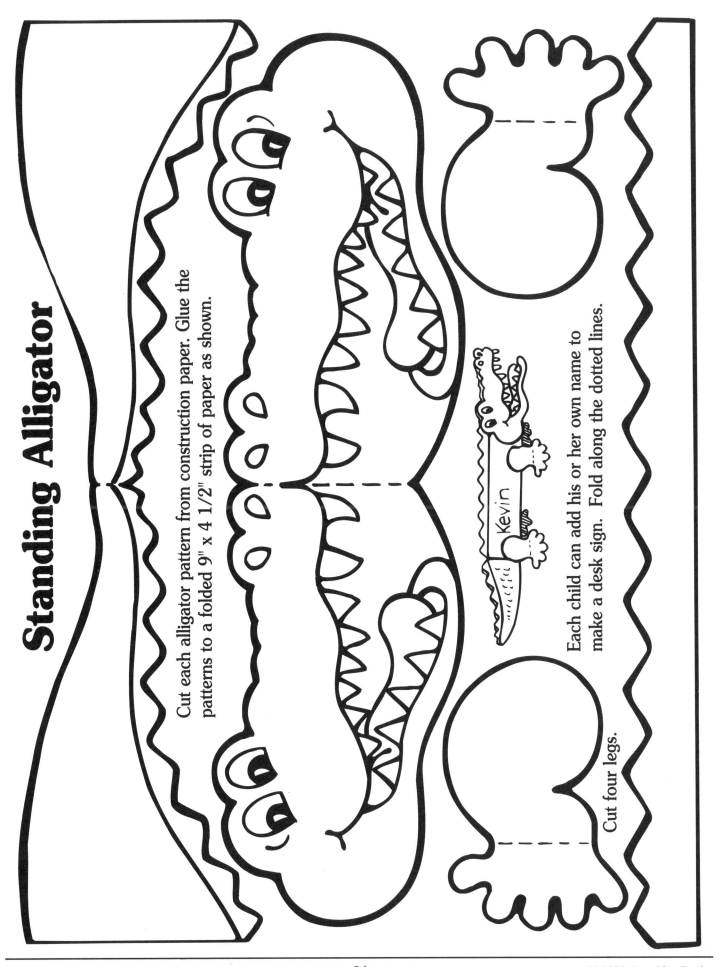

Cut each alligator pattern from construction paper. Glue the patterns to a folded 9" x 4 1/2" strip of paper as shown.

Each child can add his or her own name to make a desk sign. Fold along the dotted lines.

Kevin

Cut four legs.

Alligator Sign Topper

Cut these alligator patterns from heavy, colored paper. Use it to display student work papers or classroom announcements.

TF0600 June Idea Book

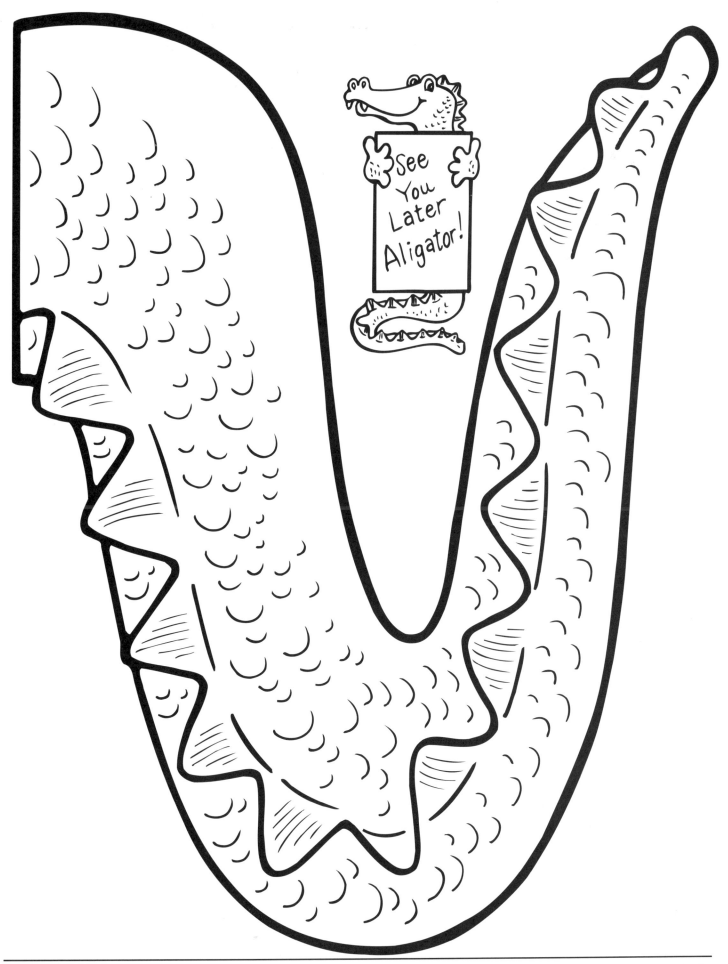

See You Later Aligator!

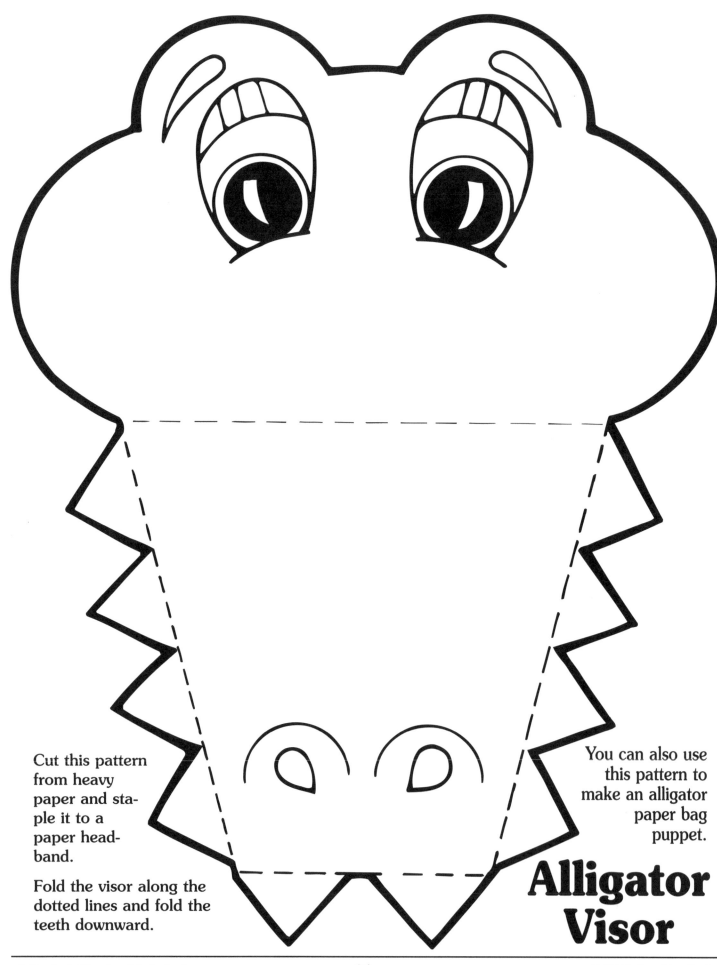

Cut this pattern from heavy paper and staple it to a paper headband.

Fold the visor along the dotted lines and fold the teeth downward.

You can also use this pattern to make an alligator paper bag puppet.

Alligator Visor

Seashore Fun!

TF0600 June Idea Book

Fishy Activities!

MATH FACT FISHING

Most children would rather go fishing than practice math facts. With this activity, they can do both!

Cut dozens of fish shapes from colored construction paper. Write a math problem on each fish. Attach a metal paper clip or safety pin to the head of each fish.

Bring in a real fishing pole from home or make one from a stick. Attach a small magnet to the end of the line. Use a decorated cardboard box as your fishing hole.

Children take turns using the pole to catch a fish. The student then reads the problem and gives an answer. If it is correct, he or she keeps the fish. If wrong, it must be thrown back. The student that catches the most fish is declared the winner.

SEASHELLS

In many areas, seashells are inexpensive and plentifu. You can pick them them up from the shore yourself or buy them in a novelty shop.

Young children will enjoy inspecting each shell and categorizing them into groups. They can also be counted, added, subtracted, etc.

Shells can also be used in a variety of art projects. A few include: gluing them on a frame for a picture, making a necklace or creating a shell and plaster of paris paper weight.

Give each student a shell to inspire their next creative writing assignment. Ask each student to speculate and write about the animal that may have lived in his or her shell.

FISH FACTS

Ask your students to research some of the more interesting facts about fish! Here are a few suggestions:

How do fish breath?
What is the largest fish?
How fast do fish swim?
How long do fish live?
How do fish sleep without eyelids?
Which fish are now extinct?
What is the most dangerous fish?
How are most fish caught?
How is pollution affecting fish?

INVENT A FISH

Ask your students to invent their own fish! When drawing a picture of it, they should use their wildest imaginations in deciding how their fish should look and what size it should be. The funnier, the better! Ask them to select an unusual name for their fish.

They may want to give some statistical information. This could be done as a creative writing assignment. Have them include information such as where it is found, what it eats, unusual characteristics, fresh water or salt water, etc.

Students will love seeing pictures of their unique fish displayed on the class bulletin board.

WHALE QUESTIONS

Ask your students to research some of these questions about whales:

• Is a whale a fish or a mammal?
• How long do most whales live?
• Which type of whale is the largest?
• Can whales hear or smell?
• Do all whales have teeth?
• What do whales eat?
• How long can a whale hold its breath?
• Which type of whale is most rare?
• What is the name for a baby whale?
• How do whales communicate with each other?
• Which whale is largest?

Fishy Activities!

OCEANOGRAPHY FIELD TRIP
A trip to the local beach or marina aquarium is great, when possible. A neighborhood pet store or local fish market however might be more convenient and nearly as educational.

At a pet store, students can see and identify a variety of fresh and saltwater fish. Workers will be happy to tell the students about the requirements the different types of fish need.

A fish market can also provide some unique opportunities. Students can see and perhaps feel clams, oysters and live lobsters. You may want to purchase some varieties of sea food to be cooked and eaten by the students. (Children will even sample small pieces of calamari (squid) or octopus, especially with a ketchup dipping sauce.)

MIGRATION MAP
California gray whales have the longest migration route of any type of mammal. They travel, round trip, approximately 11,000 miles a year!

The gray whales spend their summers in the seas of Alaska and Russia and then travel south to the lagoons of Baja California, Mexico.

Ask students to trace the gray whales' route on the class map.

PIRATE FUN!
Along with the study of oceanography, your students will love participating in a fun unit of pirate activities.

Draw a large pirate map on the class bulletin board. Students can be divided into teams and their progress charted as oceanography reports are turned in, library books read, or multiplication facts learned. Each team can race toward a large treasure chest filled with gift certificates or maybe "pieces of eight."

A scavenger hunt around the school grounds can top off the event. Then children can return to class to find buccaneer cookies and pirate grog for refreshments.

HUNTING WHALES
For hundreds of years, people have hunted and killed whales for their meat and oil. As a result, several types of whales are close to extinction.

Ask your students to research the whaling industry and how it has affected the whale population of the world. Instruct them to find out ways in which whales are harmed today. Are there still some countries that permit whaling? Are gill nets and pollution a hazard to whales?

Students may like to write to one of the following organizations:

Greenpeace
1611 Connecticut Ave., N.W.
Washington, D.C. 20009

American Cetacean Society
P.O. Box 4416
San Pedro, CA 90731

Fish Paper Bag Puppet

Fish Patterns

Curly Octopus

Cut two octopus patterns from construction paper. Turn them back-to-back and staple around the head. Curl each tentacle around a pencil and your octopus will stand up.

TF0600 June Idea Book

Octopus Arms

Assemble this octopus using a brass fastener. Cut four pairs of arms from heavy paper.

TF0600 June Idea Book

Octopus Paper Bag Puppet

TF0600 June Idea Book

Whale of a Tale!

by

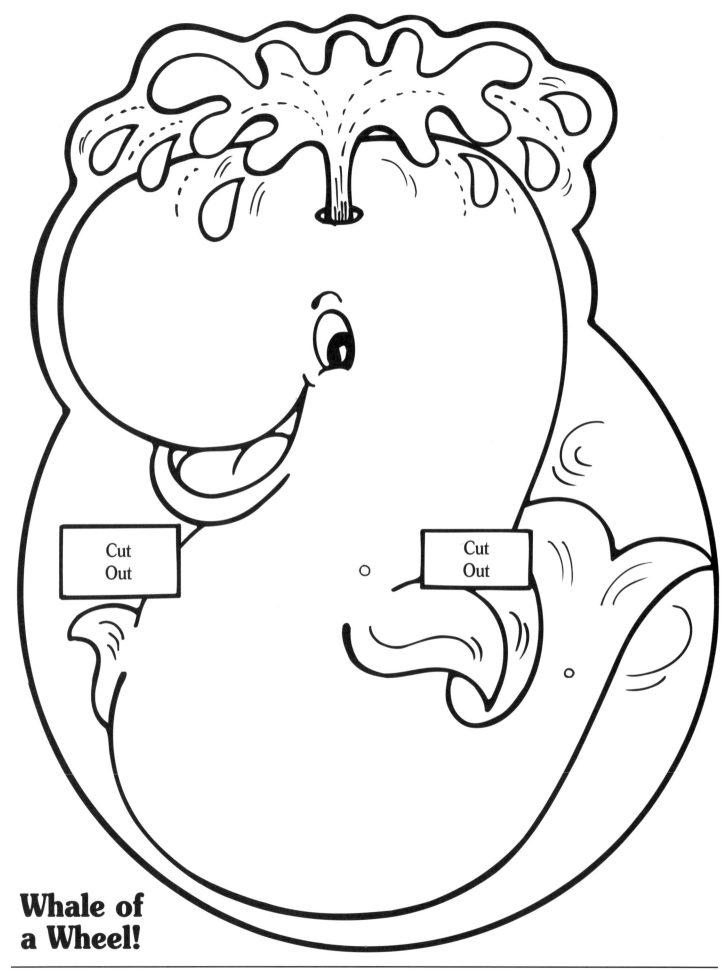

Whale of a Wheel!

TF0600 June Idea Book

Add your own math problems or word contractions to the wheel.

Move the whale's tail to reveal the correct answer.

Make a "Whale" wheel for each child in class.

TF0600 June Idea Book

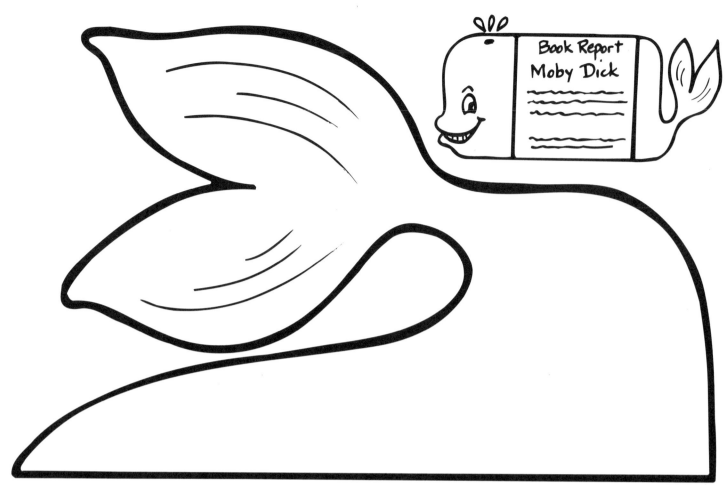

Whale of a Paper!

Cut these whale patterns from colored paper and display them around a good work paper.

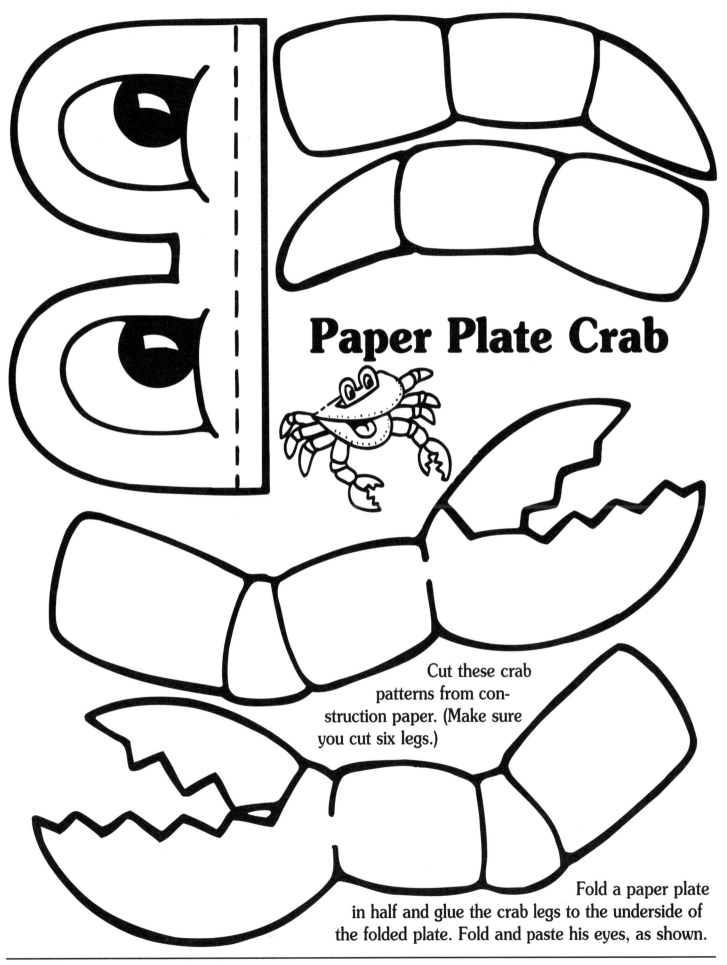

Paper Plate Crab

Cut these crab patterns from construction paper. (Make sure you cut six legs.)

Fold a paper plate in half and glue the crab legs to the underside of the folded plate. Fold and paste his eyes, as shown.

Seashore Mobile

Name _____

Cut this fish pattern and shell patterns from heavy paper. Attach a string to each seashell and hang them from the fish sign to make a fun mobile! Children can write oceanography vocabulary words on the backs of the shells.

     TF0600 June Idea Book

Seashell
Patterns

TF0600 June Idea Book

My Sea Animal Report!

Student's Name

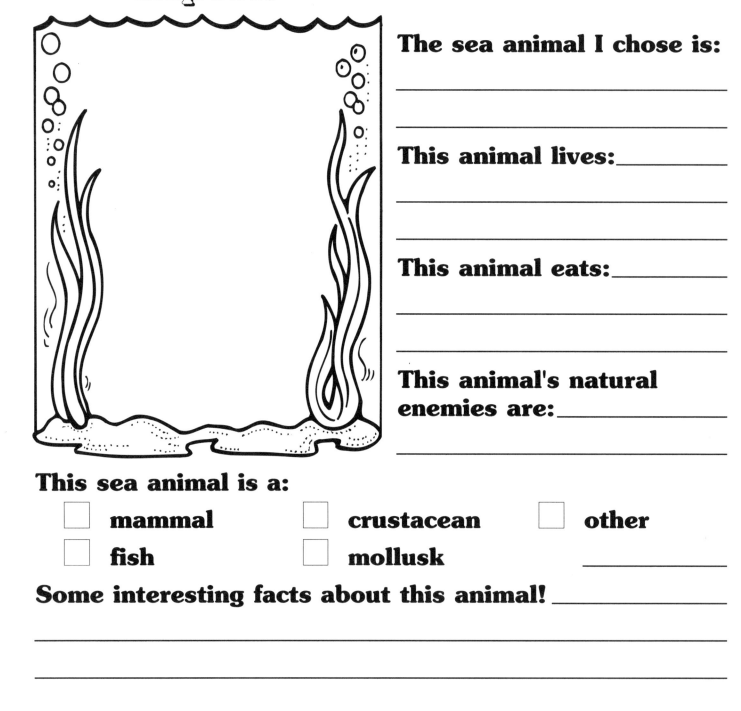

The sea animal I chose is:

_____

_____

This animal lives:_____

_____

_____

This animal eats:_____

_____

_____

This animal's natural enemies are:_____

_____

This sea animal is a:

☐ mammal   ☐ crustacean   ☐ other

☐ fish   ☐ mollusk   _____

Some interesting facts about this animal! _____

_____

_____

_____

_____

_____

Shark Pattern

Cut these shark patterns form colored paper. Display them around a sheet of 9" x 12" construction paper. Write classroom rules, upcoming event information or student helper names on the sheet of paper. A great way to show off good work papers!

Mermaid Pattern

Have students make their own mermaids to display around creative writing assignments. Glitter can be used to decorate her tail and hair after students have colored her with crayons or markers.

113

TF0600 June Idea Book

Fishy Crafts!

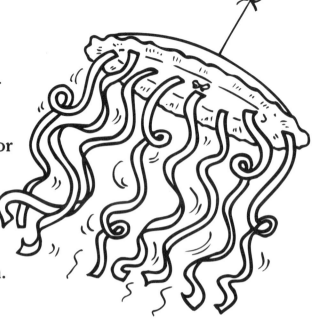

JELLYFISH CRAFT!

Students will love making these colorful jelly-fish!

Cut long, thin strips of colored tissue paper or use gift wrap ribbon to make the tentacles for each jellyfish. Flue one end of each ribbon or strip to the underside of a paper plate. When dry, attach a string and hang the jellyfish from the ceiling of the classroom.

FISH POCKETS!

Create a school of fish on the class bulletin board as a way for students to collect and display awards and notes of completion.

Give each student one and one-half paper plates. Instruct them to staple the half plate to the whole plate to form a pocket. Students can cut fish heads, tails and fins from construction paper and glue the pieces to the paper plates to make each fish. Decorate the board with a sandy bottom and paper seaweed. Award the students with paper bubbles that can be placed in the fish pockets as they are earned!

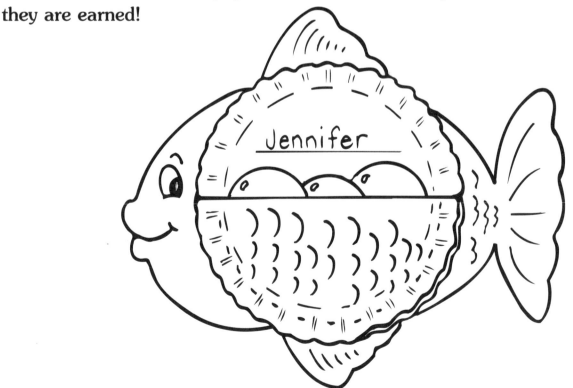

Creative Writing Fish!

Sea Animal List

Use these sea animal names in a variety of activities. Children can sort them into categories or select one on which to do a report. You can also use them to play bingo.

jellyfish	sailfish	tiger shark
flounder	halibut	starfish
seahorse	oyster	clam
sponge	eel	crab
lobster	manta ray	harbor seal
dolphin	blue whale	octopus
shrimp	grey whale	porpoise
killer whale	sea turtle	hammerhead
swordfish	squid	herring
lionfish	barracuda	mussel
triggerfish	sea urchin	yellowtail
black seabass	grouper	bass
blue marlin	mackerel	scallop
humpback whale	anchovy	salmon
sardine	tuna	sunfish
sea otter	clownfish	sea anemone
great white shark	sperm whale	cod

TF0600 June Idea Book

Fishbowl

Give each student a copy of this fish-
bowl pattern. Instruct them to decorate
the bowl by drawing sandy water plants
and maybe shells or rocks. Cover the
bowl with a piece of clear plastic wrap,
leaving an opening in the top. Students
can earn paper fish that can then be
placed in the fishbowls.

The South Pacific!

The South Pacific Islands!

There are thousands of islands scattered across the Pacific Ocean. No one knows exactly how many, but it is estimated at more than 20,000. Some islands are very large and cover thousands of square miles, while others are very tiny and barely rise above water level.

The cultures, customs, weather, geography and economies of the islands differ greatly. The Pacific Islands are divided into three main groups.

Melanesia (meaning black islands) - includes New Guinea, the Solomon Islands, New Caledonia and Fiji.

Micronesia (meaning tiny islands) - includes the islands north of the equator such as Guam, the Caroline Islands, the Marshall Islands and the island of Nauru.

Polynesia (meaning many islands) - occupies the largest area of the South Pacific. Most of the islands are included in this group including the Hawaiian Islands, Tahiti, Samoa, New Zealand and Easter Island.

Invite someone who is from one of the South Pacific Islands or someone that has visited many of the islands to speak to your class. Encourage them to bring in photos, postcards, handicrafts and souvenirs that they may have collected to show to the students. (You may be able to find someone who can demonstrate the hula or a traditional Tahitian dance.

Island Activities!

ISLAND VOCABULARY

Ask your students to use some of these words in a creative writing assignment about the Pacific Islands. Some of the words may be given as research assignments.

ALOHA	PLANTATION
CARIBBEAN	POI
EQUATOR	POLYNESIA
HULA	SUGAR CANE
ISLAND	SURF
LEI	TOURIST
LUAU	TRADE WINDS
NATIVE	TREASURE
OCEAN	TROPICAL
PALM	VOLCANO

CREATIVE ISLANDS

Ask your students to imagine that they have just discovered an uncharted island. Suggest that they invite tourists to their island by means of developing a travel brochure. On the brochure they should include the following:

Name of the island
Interesting features
Weather and climate
Available activities
Location

Students can also illustrate pictures for their brochure. They may want to show the island's most famous attractions, flag and map.

Island Activities!

ISLAND FOODS

Let your students sample a variety of exotic foods from the Islands. Here are some suggestions:

Pineapple - Have small children examine a fresh pineapple, feeling its rough and prickly skin. Show them how you test for a pineapple's ripeness by easily removing one of the center leaves. Cut it in half and explain that the center core and the rough skin are inedible. Cut into chunks and let your students sample its goodness.

Coconut - Pass around a coconut in its husk and ask your students to describe how it feels. Drain the milk by poking a hole into one of the coconut's soft spots. With the milk drained, crack the husk with a hammer. Give each student a small piece to sample. Students will also like to taste the milk.

Papaya and Mango - Let your students examine these two tropical fruits before you cut them into pieces and let them have a taste. Ask the children to describe their taste and texture. Can they think of any other food or fruit that has a similar taste?

Sugar Cane - An important export of most tropical areas is sugar. Without telling your students what it is, give each of them a small piece of sugar cane and ask them to chew the inside pulp.

Dates and Macadamia Nuts - These two foods might be a bit costly but well worth the effort when discussing the foods of the islands.

HAWAII

Ask your students to find out about our 50th state. Here are some research suggestions:

• Find out about the weather in Hawaii.
• Find out how islands are formed.
• Find out when Hawaii became a state, the name of the first governor and the capital city.
• Find out how many islands make up the state of Hawaii and draw a map of them.
• Find out about Hawaii's most important crops.
• Find out about one of Hawaii's famous volcanoes.
• Find out about the Hawaiian people and who first discovered the islands.

PIZZA ISLANDS

Make a classroom pizza that's even more fun to make than it is to eat!

Using a boxed pizza mix, shape the dough on a greased cookie sheet in the shape of one or more islands. (You might want to use a map of Hawaii as a model.)

Children can add sauce for vegetation and grated parmesan cheese for sand. They can also add mushrooms for boats and olives for villages and cities. Children will love using their imaginations for other things they can add to the island pizzas. Bake and serve. What a fun way to end a unit on islands!

Pacific
Islands

Pacific Islands

Island Crafts!

HAWAIIAN LEIS

Cut colored tissue paper into four inch squares. Take three or four sheets and fold them into quarters. Cut into a flower shape using the pattern. Cut an "X" in the center of each flower with an art knife.

Using a length of yarn, carefully thread the flowers along the yarn. The tissue flowers will stay in place without glue or tape. Arrange the flowers along the yarn and tie the two ends together to make the lei.

HULA SKIRTS

Ask students to bring to class several large, brown grocery bags. Cut the bags into long one inch strips. Using a length of heavy yarn, loop one end of each paper strip around the yarn and glue or staple in place. When finished, tie the skirt around your waist.

Boys may prefer to make wrap-around skirts from brown butcher paper that they can wear over shorts. Cut the paper wide enough to wrap around the waist. Children can use crayons to draw island symbols and decorations. Cut a slit up one side of the skirt and tape to hold in place.

Flamingos!

Display a row of pink flamingos on the class board, each labeled with a student's name. Cut long strips of colored paper for the flamingo's legs. Add a beach scene, palm trees and a setting sun to create the atmosphere of an island paradise.

Treasure Chest

Have each student cut a treasure chest from construction paper. The lid can be fastened with a brass fastener.

Reward student with gold paper coins. Students could also draw their own treasure inside the chest and then write a story about it.

TF0600 June Idea Book

Pirate Costume

Cut two pirate hat patterns from folded black construction paper and paste the skull-and-crossbones in the center of one of them. Staple the corners of the hat together to fit your head.

The eye patch is also cut from black paper. Punch out the two holes and fasten with black string. Cut the earring from colored or metallic paper. Fasten it to your ear by fitting the open end over your earlobe.

Children will love wearing their pirate costume on a special "Swashbuckler Day."

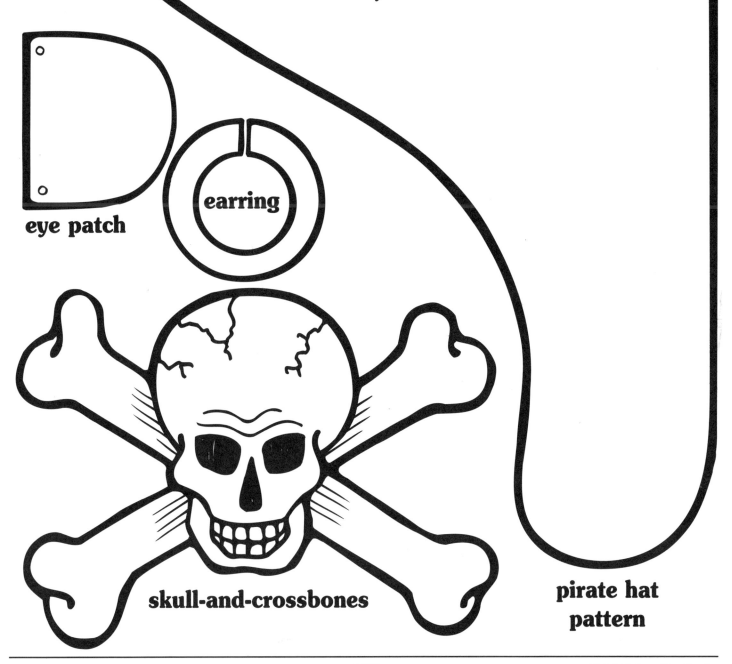

eye patch

earring

skull-and-crossbones

pirate hat
pattern

 TF0600 June Idea Book

Treasure Hunt

TEACHERS: Make your own task cards and use this gameboard to reinforce your students' knowledge.

TF0600 June Idea Book

Gameboard!

My Story of Hidden Treasure!

by: _____

_____

_____

_____

_____

_____

_____

_____

_____

_____

_____

_____

_____

Pirate Patterns

Children can use these pirate patterns to display their treasure hunt stories.

Treasure Hunt!

TF0600 June Idea Book

Island Symbols

TF0600 June Idea Book

Bulletin Boards and More!

TREASURES
In Room 12!

Diane Freddie Richie Manuel Susan Paula Mike Rosie

TF0600 June Idea Book

Bulletin Boards and More!

LEAP INTO LEARNING!

Paper bag frog puppets will leap off the bulletin board with this clever idea. Ask each student to make their own frog puppet and display the best ones on the board along with paper lily pads and cattails.

OCTOPUS HELPERS!

Display a large paper octopus on the class bulletin board with the title "Octopus Helpers."

Label each arm with a classroom job. Write each student's name on a 3 x 5 card and place it in the grasp of an the appropriate arm. Each week, rotate the cards to other arms to change the jobs.

You could also use this cute idea to display reading groups or classroom teams.

FRIENDSHIP

Emphasize respect for one another by displaying this striking "hands" bulletin board. Enlarge the hands, as shown, using butcher paper. Or, you may wish to make a chain of clasping hands reaching from one end of the room to the other.

Bulletin Boards and More!

WE'RE MATH SHARKS

Cut several sharks from colored butcher paper. Write word problems on each shark that pertain to these fascinating sea creatures. One example might be: "If this shark eats 30 pounds of fish a day, how much does it eat in one week?" Students can write their answers on the air bubbles.

START A SUMMER HOBBY!

Cut a giant sun from yellow butcher paper and pin it to the bulletin board. Ask students to list different hobbies that they might enjoy doing this summer.

Write the various hobbies around the sun, as shown.

TERRIFIC TURTLES!

Display a large paper turtle on the class board as a way to keep students motivated.

Cut a variety of colorful shapes, labeled with student names, and pin them to the turtle's shell. Stickers or stars can be placed on the shapes when students improve behavior or accomplish goals.

You may want to give each student their own paper turtle. Shapes on the turtle's shell can be colored in as assignments are completed.

Bulletin Boards and More!

ISLAND HOPPING!

Inspire students to accomplish tasks promptly with an "Island Hopping" theme.

Have each student make a sailboat from construction paper and label it with his or her name. Cover the class bulletin board with blue paper and place a number of paper islands around the board. Label each island with a weekly task. The students move their sailboats from island to island until they again reach the mainland. Once there, they receive a gold star or sticker that is placed on their boat. Then, the journey begin again!

CATCH A BIG ONE!

Cover the class bulletin board with blue paper. Label each student's name across the top of the board. Attach a string to each name. Cut large, colorful paper fish and attach them to each child's hook. Use the fish pattern on page 115. These fish can denote classroom jobs or reading groups.

You might also want to use this same idea to reward classroom achievements. Stickers or gold stars can be applied to the individual fish.

SPOUTING THE BEST!

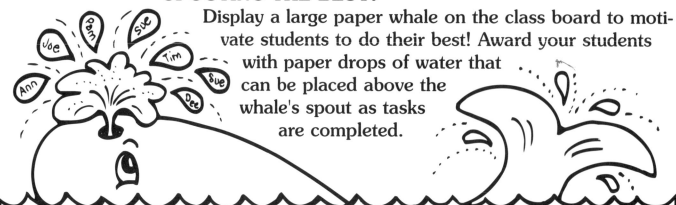

Display a large paper whale on the class board to motivate students to do their best! Award your students with paper drops of water that can be placed above the whale's spout as tasks are completed.

Sneaky Snake

Enlarge or copy this snake pattern on colored butcher paper. Make it as long as you wish.

Write rules or students' names along its body and display on the class board.

Fisherman Pattern

Have students write "fishy" stories using the fish pattern on page 115. Hang the fish stories from a string tied to the end of this fisherman's pole.

Friendship Hands

Shark

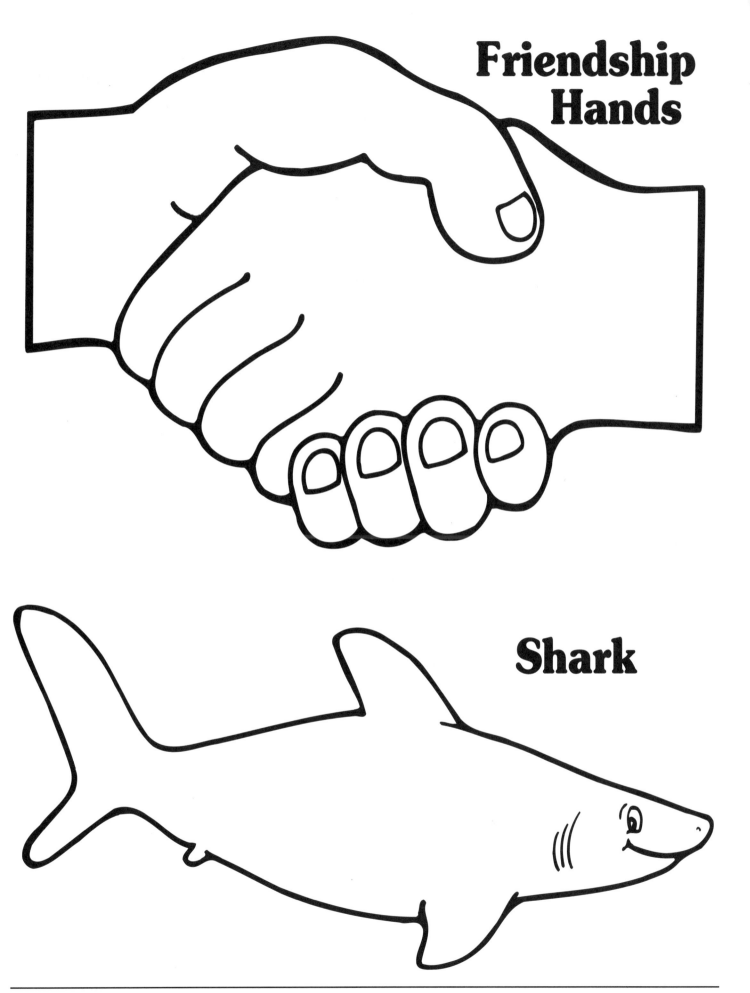

Al E. Gator

Enlarge "Al" onto colored butcher paper. Make his tail as long as you like.
Use him to display the alphabet, numerals, or a classroom announcement.

TF0600 June Idea Book

Fish Paper Topper

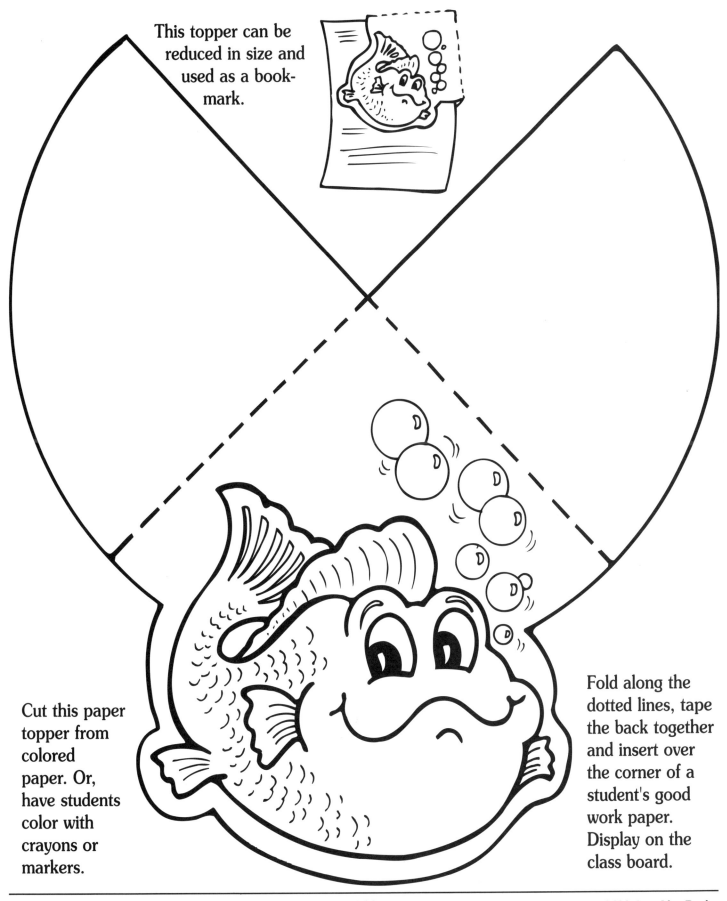

This topper can be reduced in size and used as a bookmark.

Cut this paper topper from colored paper. Or, have students color with crayons or markers.

Fold along the dotted lines, tape the back together and insert over the corner of a student's good work paper. Display on the class board.

Picture Frame

This picture frame can be used in a variety of ways. Cut it from heavy paper or posterboard. You might also cut it from gold or silver paper to create a gilded frame. Here are some ideas:

- Enlarge the pattern to make the frame fit a student's good work paper. Acknowledge one student each day by framing his or her work.

- Let each student draw a self-portrait in the center of the frame pattern. Display all the portraits on the class board during "Back to School" activities.

- Reduce the size of the frame and have each student paste his or her school photo in the center. Back the frame with a square of posterboard. Paste a folded triangle of posterboard to the back to make the frame stand on a table.

My Wish for a Great Summer!

Name

TF0600 June Idea Book

Answer Key!

ACTIVITY 1

Crossword:

1. S
4. W A T E R
   I
   M
5. A R M S   6. L E G S
   M   2. L   O
7. L I F E G U A R D
   N   A   T
   G   P

3. F L O A T

ACTIVITY 2

```
S C V G F (S W I M) K L O P L K J H F T Y
L A W E D F R S D R F T L D E R F G H Y
E S (C O O K) S D F G T Y A D (S P O R T S)
E S W E R A E S W D F R Y W S T Y U I O
P A E D R F W (E X P L O R E) D T Y U K M
I S W (G A R D E N) D G T Y H (B O A T E R)
C W Q E R T Y U A W E R T Y H G F D S T
N F R T Y U H J H D F T Y G H U I J K L
I D R F G T I F (F I S H) F T Y U I O P V
C (B I K E) D K V G T Y H N M K I O L R E
A X C G T Y E (C A M P) D V G T Y H N M J
A W E D S C F R T G B H Y U J M N K I O
A S D F G Y Y H J K I O (S K A T E) D R T
X C Z V B G F D S A Z X B N M J K H F D
```

ACTIVITY 3

leturt	**t u r t l e**
skena	**s n a k e**
grof	**f r o g**
adot	**t o a d**
toraglila	**a l l i g a t o r**
zildar	**l i z a r d**
colideroc	**c r o c o d i l e**
trtooise	**t o r t o i s e**

ACTIVITY 4

1. Frogs start life as <u>t a d p o l e s</u>.
2. Frogs and toads are <u>a m p h i b i a n s</u>.
3. Most water turtles are <u>m e a t</u> eaters.
4. Land turtles are <u>p l a n t</u> eaters.
5. Some tortoises can live to be <u>1 0 0</u> years old.
6. All turtles lay <u>e g g s</u>.
7. All reptiles are <u>c o l d</u> -blooded.
8. Snakes have no <u>l e g s</u>.
9. Turtles, crocodiles, lizards and snakes are <u>r e p t i l e s</u>.